"*Getting It Write* by Lee Zahavi Jessup, a beloved ind
of the question: How do you become a working writ... ... ...... ....... .......
success stories of writers she's worked with and gives the writer an insider's look
at what it takes to make the sale. There is no stone left unturned."

  —Jen Grisanti, Story/Career Consultant, Writing Instructor for Writers on the Verge
   at NBC, Author of *Change Your Story, Change Your Life* and *Story Line*

"Writing a screenplay just for fun is one thing... but if you really want to turn
it into a career, you can't go wrong with Ms. Jessup's wonderful book.
Enter Hollywood with a clear focus and avoid the inevitable pitfalls that have
stalled too many careers."

  —Matthew Terry, Filmmaker, Screenwriter, Teacher; Reviewer for *microfilmmaker.com*

"*Getting It Write* will shatter all your excuses, and provide you with
insightful revelations about what today's Hollywood looks for and expects
in a screenwriter."

  —Michael Hauge, Hollywood Story and Script Consultant;
   Author of *Writing Screenplays That Sell* and *Selling Your Story in 60 Seconds*

"Lee's wisdom from years of experience takes you from simply being a writer in
a cave to arming you with the knowledge you need to improve your odds of
success. A must-read book for all up-and-coming writers who are serious about
their screenwriting careers."

  —Jeanne Veillette Bowerman, Screenwriter; Editor, *Script Magazine*

"When you read Lee's book, you gain real-world, practical information to help
move your screenwriting career forward, and will walk out with a real strategy."

  —Pilar Alessandra, On the Page

"Lee Zahavi Jessup is a screenwriter's 'career midwife.' She is your caring ally in her
book, helping you overcome uncertainty and push toward fulfilling your creative
dreams."

  —Academy Award–nominated filmmaker Pen Densham, *Robin Hood: Prince of Thieves*,
   *Backdraft*, *Moll Flanders*, and *Phantom* with Ed Harris and David Duchovny

"Tangible, real, and inspiring. Lee knows the industry, how it's changed, and
what works. Invaluable for all screenwriters."

  —Dave Watson, Editor, Movies Matter

"Lee Zahavi Jessup has laid out a detailed map of the expansive landscape available to screenwriters trying to sell their first scripts and build a career. This is not a how-to book on writing; it is a practical and inspiring guide to getting screenplays read by the people who can buy them."
 —Bob Gebert, Screenwriter

"*Getting It Write* is the perfect starting point for anyone trying to get his or her screenwriting career off the ground. I wish it had been available back when I first started representing writers. It should be required reading for every aspiring screenwriter."
 —Jason Scoggins, Founder, *SpecScout.com*

"Lee helps writers map out a path to success, including a realistic look at the services and events marketed to new writers. This book is an up-to-date guide explaining the realities of breaking in with enough encouragement to keep you from being overwhelmed by the prospect of making writing your career."
 —Shelly Mellott, VP Events and Services, Final Draft;
 Founding Editor, *Script Magazine*

"Lee's lifetime of industry experience puts the gold seal of authenticity on every word of advice. If you're serious about writing movies for a living... this book is a must-read."
 —Dwayne Alexander Smith, Author, *Ten Simple F\*cking Rules to Writing a Great F\*cking Screenplay* and the novel *Forty Acres*

"Finally a book that fully answers the universal question every screenwriter asks upon tightening the screws on their screenplay: Now what?"
 —Richard Botto, Founder, CEO Stage 32 and optioned Screenwriter

"If your goal is to make it as a screenwriter, *Getting It Write* should be on your bookshelf! Whether you're just starting out or facing a writing career block, screenwriters are sure to find the advice and strategies to propel them ahead!"
 —Kathie Fong Yoneda,  Script Consultant, Workshop Leader,
 Author of *The Script-Selling Game*

# Getting It
# WRITE

An Insider's Guide To

## A SCREENWRITING CAREER

## LEE ZAHAVI JESSUP

Coolidge
*CAREER*
*808.2*
*ZaRavi*
*2014*

Published by Michael Wiese Productions

12400 Ventura Blvd., #1111

Studio City, CA 91604

tel. 818.379.8799

fax 818.986.3408

mw@mwp.com

www.mwp.com

3 1712 01489 7691

Cover Design: John Brenner (www.johnnyink.com)
Book Design: Gina Mansfield Design
Copyeditor: Gary Sunshine

Printed by McNaughton & Gunn, Inc., Saline, Michigan
Manufactured in the United States of America

Library of Congress Cataloging-in-Publication Data

Zahavi, Lee Jessup.
  Getting it write : an insider's guide to a screenwriting career / Lee Jessup Zahavi.
    pages cm
  ISBN 978-1-61593-175-0
  1. Motion picture authorship. I. Title.
  PN1996.Z35 2014
  8058.2'3023--dc23
                        2013046040

MIX
Paper from
responsible sources
FSC® C011935

# TABLE OF CONTENTS

# DEDICATION

*Finding oneself solidly between gratitude and humility is not a bad place to be.
In that spirit, I would like to take this opportunity to commit some appreciation
to paper:*

*To the entire team at Culver City's Akasha Café who welcomed me day
in and day out as I hulled up at the corner table with my Mac, an Earl Grey
tea and the occasional macaroon indulgence, taking client meetings
and working on this book.*

*To Dan Sherlock, my shepherd.*

*To Kris Paider, my longest-standing client and dearest friend.
This is your fault, darling. I am eternally in your debt.*

*To Kelly Anelons, ongoing source of insight, inspiration, and laughter,
who in her own way guided me to where I am today.*

*To my fearless mother, and her eternal, contagious faith that,
against all odds, things will work out in the most glorious way.*

*To my rock of a father, who taught me to dream big and never fear
putting it all on the line when things really matter.*

*Together, you two encouraged me to take chances most parents would deem
reckless. I couldn't be more grateful for your love, trust, and guidance.*

*To my Lennon and Lula, whose beauty, magic, and brilliance
I could never put into words, and who inspire me every day.*

*And to my amazing Tony, who is brave when I can't be, strong where
I am weak, and still manages to see me in the best light even when I am
at my worst... None of this would have happened without you. And, let's
face it, even if it did, without you it wouldn't have mattered.*

# FOREWORD
## Taking Charge of Your Screenwriting Career

When I sat down to write this book, Kelly, my client and friend who started on this road with me many years ago on a rainy day in Boston, emailed me: *"Didn't I tell you no one wrote this book before?"*

This book doesn't deliver a three-step formula for selling your screenplay and making a million bucks. If such a formula existed, it would have been committed to paper a long time before now. Instead, it provides real tools, insight, and knowledgeable advice for writers tired of writing script after script without success or forward progress on the career front, and offers real, actionable solutions to help you build, brick by deliberate brick, the screenwriting career you've been dreaming about.

The one-and-done model of screenwriting, in which you would write a screenplay, stimulate a bidding war, sell the script, and fade into obscurity is, for the most part, gone. Today's market favors writers who can continuously produce stellar ideas and high-quality content. Therefore, my approach is NOT screenplay focused. It is career focused; putting weight on the development of the screenwriter's career over any one screenplay.

Building a screenwriting career doesn't happen overnight. But new writers are breaking in every day, and thereby prove, practically, realistically, and without much fanfare, that it can, indeed, be done. Just days before I started writing this foreword, an item came out on *Deadline.com* about a writer who, that week, went from waiter to studio scribe. He had an agent in place, and a script named to The Black List the year prior, but was still making a living as a waiter when the studio deal was struck. Which goes to prove: armed with knowledge and willing to put in the work, new writers are breaking in all the time. Do I need to say it again? *New writers are working hard and breaking in all the time.* But if it's an easy road you're looking for, the snap of a finger, a fairy tale in which you send your script to a single industry executive and become a screenwriting sensation overnight, this book is not for you.

If you think that networking, branding, pitching skills, and industry know-how are nowhere near a necessity for making a real go of your screenwriting career, put this book back on the shelf. Turn off your Kindle or iPad. Walk away. This is not for you. It will likely only piss you off.

Still here?

Great.

The hoops that new writers are made to jump through in today's marketplace are there not to make your life hard, but rather to separate unskilled amateurs from talented, promising, aspiring professionals trying to make a real go of this screenwriting stuff. The belief is that if you are indeed serious about taking the plunge and making a go of your screenwriting career, you will educate yourself and take the right steps that will get you noticed and your screenplay in the spotlight.

This book is written for those who no longer want to hear the old cliché, which sounds nice but helps no one: just write a good script and everything will work out. The industry will miraculously show up. This book that I wrote for Kelly, and Kris, and Leigh, and Ted, and Liane, and John, and Jocelyne, and Melissa (and the other Melissa), and Chas, and Brendan, and Alex, and Susan, and Robyn, and Mike, and all three Jennifers, and Jim, and Joey, and Michelle, and Nevada and many, many others, is written for screenwriters who are ready to take the plunge. To put away the romance of how they thought their screenwriting career would, could, or should happen, and instead start making real, informed strides toward the career they've been dreaming about. Building a screenwriting career takes talent, tenacity, passion, and industry know-how. Armed with those assets and willing to work consistently toward the goal you have in mind, you will find that your screenwriting career will be very much within your grasp.

# INTRODUCTION
Lee Zahavi Jessup, Screenwriting Career Coach

As a little girl, a movie set was my playground. My favorite place to go. Better than any summer camp or high-end mall.

When I was ten, my father, following years of editing late-night network news, plunged back into his passion — film production. Making movies was what he gladly gave up in order to spend time with me once I was born. When he delved back into his true love, filmmaking, he generously brought me along. From casting to the movies' promotional taglines, I was allowed to participate in it all. Straight from school, I would skip my way to the set, where I was assigned daily jobs with different departments: paperwork with the assistant directors, learning equipment with the grips, studying the boards with the soundman.

But nothing got me more than story: scrutinizing the inner workings of material, understanding structure, and breaking down the arc of each character. That stuff was gold. My father gave me my first script to analyze when I was just ten years old. Some families talk politics and sports around the dinner table; we passionately argued movies. Still do.

When I was eleven, my father took me to see *Flashdance*. Walking home, we got into a heated discussion.

"What is the movie about?" he asked.

"Dancing," I said.

But still, he pressed, what was the movie really about? We talked and talked until we narrowed it down to a single line:

If you lose your dream, you're dead.

That, I could easily get behind.

I was hooked.

When I became a young adult my father was resolute that I build my career on my own. To prove myself, I landed my first production job not one year out of high school and for a number of years was a production gypsy, living job to job. Production took me to Asia, Africa, Europe. Like many aspiring filmmakers trying to figure out their path, I wrote a screenplay, then got lucky when a thriving production company optioned the material. The company had a studio deal. William Morris (now WME) was packaging the project for us. It was, for the simplest of reasons, the greatest gift I could have gotten: it allowed me to realize at a young age that, despite any innate talent, being a working screenwriter was just not what I wanted to do with my life. My heart lay in screenplay development much more than generating content or spending years in film production. And so I jumped headfirst into a development job. Story, writers, analysis, all of those fell seamlessly into my sweet spot.

But despite my best hopes, development was not an easy job. I felt an immense responsibility to those whose projects my company took on. Every screenplay I fell in love with became a dream I desperately needed to see come true. Each project that failed to make it felt like a personal failure.

What's a girl to do? In my late twenties, it came time to give a real-world job a shot. A job that wouldn't keep me up nights aching over letting down the very artists I wanted to support. But my grandmother always warned me, "A person plans, and God laughs." Which, incidentally, sounds much better in Yiddish. One year into my perfectly vanilla corporate job running sales and marketing for an Internet company powering the industry's premier information database, an unexpected opportunity dropped in my lap: the chance to run *ScriptShark.com*, one of the company's web properties and the leading online coverage destination. No matter how far from film development I thought the job I took was, the universe clearly had other plans for me.

At *ScriptShark* I spent my days shepherding the screenplays that came across my desk. Within two years, and with lots of personal attention, the business had grown by 123%. Part of my job was identifying material ready for market, and connecting qualified writers with agents, managers, and potential production partners. Hundreds of screenplays came my way every year, but only 4% of those, at best, were ready to share with my industry colleagues. Nonetheless, each time one of my qualifying writers got noticed by the right people, be they development executives, agents, managers, or producers, I did a little happy dance in my cramped office.

Getting executives to notice the work is one thing; translating a little attention into an actual career is another. For every writer who got represented or optioned, I saw dozens who did not know how to conduct themselves in a business environment. Some lead with their desperation; they needed to be validated, needed to know that their dream was going to come true. Others clearly did not know their role, arrived to meetings unprepared, expected to receive too much too soon.

So after having seen one too many talented writers write a great script but blow it on the business front, I launched a national seminar in collaboration with Final Draft and sponsored by the *New York Times*, dedicated to educating scribes on the business aspects of their chosen careers.

Let's be perfectly clear: getting a job in the industry is no ordinary employment scenario. Gone are the days when one could send in a screenplay and six to ten weeks later receive a check. These days, being a screenwriter is a high-visibility, high-involvement, high-competition, high-returns job. You have to understand the story AND know the business, having a firm grasp on the inner workings of it all. Professionals want to work with other professionals. The key is pursuing your career with purpose, clarity, and focus.

The seminar grew rapidly, taking me to major cities beyond Los Angeles — New York, Chicago, Boston, Seattle. I discovered that because there is no secret sauce to success, most consultants focused on elements they could formulate. Screenplay development. Pitching. Presentation. Me? I wanted to help writers figure out how to construct a long-standing career rather than get momentarily noticed.

I met hundreds of screenwriters hungry to parlay their creative passion into working success. Soon, scribes from across the country reached out to me for guidance. And before I knew it, I had a handful of very passionate, determined, hardworking clients.

My clients quickly became my staunchest career advocates: "You should quit your day job." "Go legit." "Become a screenwriting career coach full time." And, with a little bit of guidance, they were raking in worthwhile accomplishments themselves: One had become a bestselling author. A writing team was actively developing their screenplay with a prominent New York production company. Yet another was a finalist in Final Draft's Big Break contest.

Short of watching my kids grow, I had never been more proud.

Soon, I left the corporate job and never looked back.

Now, my coaching clients include WGA members, Emmy- and Golden Globe–nominated scribes, screenwriting aspirants and produced screenwriters, sold screenwriters, represented screenwriters, contest winners and even a screenwriting guru. I conduct webinars, interviews, and podcasts with the industry's leading screenwriting brands, and have traveled as far as Paris to speak to writers eager to turn writing into a career.

And every day that I get to do this, I thank my lucky stars. I love my job.

I am in the business of helping people. I spent years gathering the knowledge that makes me an effective career coach. Part cheerleader, part drill sergeant, part strategist, I am in the business of helping writers turn their dreams into working realities, of championing, guiding, and supporting scribes as they become fulfilled by progressing with purpose and focus toward making their passions come alive.

Chapter One

# GROUND RULES

A writer once emailed me: *"I'm a busy mother of two with a high-profile job. I just finished writing a great screenplay (my first one!) but I don't have any desire to hustle to get people reading it or to find representation. What do you think about me putting up a website with my screenplay, for producers and agents to find and read online?"*

The problem with industry executives, be they producers, development executives, or representation executives, is that they are very busy people with scripts coming at them from every direction. Rarely are they trolling the Web in the hopes of clicking their way onto their next success.

Building a screenwriting career used to be different way back when. You could sit in your apartment, punching your script out on an old Remington at any hour of the day. The script would make its way into an envelope marked HOLLYWOOD, and six to ten weeks later, voila! If your script were in any way desirable, you'd find a check in the mail. Many a writer, Ayn Rand among them, got their start this way. Nowadays, in order for you to achieve screenwriting success, you have to understand the value you bring to the marketplace, thoughtfully craft your voice and brand, and present your work in a deliberate, compelling, thought-out way.

Like any other dynamic field of business, the entertainment industry is a bustling place. Sure, *Entourage* may have made it look like fun and games, but writers, filmmakers, and executives alike are all expected to build their success on the back of hard work.

To make sure you don't process the term "Hard Work" in an ambiguous way, let's outline in broad strokes what it's going to take:

- Always Be Writing. — Actively, continuously, on an ongoing basis. The more you write, the better you will get. It's as simple as that. Your third script will be better than your first; the fifth better than your third. As a working professional, it's your job to continuously come up with exciting new work.

- Writing is only half the game. — In today's competitive climate, being a great writer is where it starts, but not where it ends. You are expected to recognize how your material fits within the marketplace, have a strong grasp on how the industry works, and a clear understanding of the business side of a screenwriter's career, from branding to representation and onward.

- Make a name for yourself. — Through contest wins, networking, and strong word of mouth, get word about your fantastic screenplay out there. The industry will pay attention. But you will have to do the work on an ongoing basis for it to translate to a tangible screenwriting career.

Not sure how to accomplish all of this? Keep reading, and we will get there, step by valuable step.

## Launching and Sustaining Your Screenwriting Career

Let's establish some ground rules, some agreed-upon truths before we get started:

- It's possible. — Often I meet writers who tell me that their screenwriting career is doomed before it's even begun. They don't know anyone. They live outside of Hollywood. They are past their prime. Let's be perfectly clear: IT IS ENTIRELY POSSIBLE. People without previous connections or industry pedigree, local to Los Angeles or living remotely, break in every day. But it takes ongoing, consistent dedication to achieve any level of sustainable success.

- But it's not easy. — Seriously. Like I said in the Foreword, if you're looking for three easy steps to screenwriting success, you might as well put the book down and walk away.

- From here on out, it's in your hands. — I've seen writers from Kentucky get representation, scribes from Seattle option their work. I've met writers in Chicago and Minnesota who are working every day. I know inept authors who figured out how to pitch, and anxious scribes win over management. Your screenwriting success will be directly related to how far you're willing to push yourself.

Your success will have as much to do with your attitude as it will your craft. Here are a few guidelines to keep in mind in the professional space:

- Be nice. To everyone. — You never know who is on the other end of the line or where that person will end up some day. A studio head in ten years may be an intern today. So be nice to everyone without discriminating. It will make your life much easier.

- No one likes a victim. — Even if you wholeheartedly believe your screenwriting partner screwed you over, your agent sold you out, or a studio stole your work, unless you're ready to take it to court, at least initially, keep it to yourself. No one likes to work with a victim, and others will fear you will eventually turn that attitude toward them.

- Being real goes a long way. — The entertainment industry is a highly social environment. Once you start working, you will spend months, even years toiling on a project with a team. Don't try to become who you think they want you to be; in order to build long-term success you will have to find comfort

*Television producers and showrunners* will want to work with you if they are convinced your talent and experience will bring a valuable voice and an expert, speedy hand to their existing show, and that you will work collaboratively with the team around you.

It may be personal to you; to everyone else it's about building a business relationship that makes sense.

## Industry Terms

Here is a list of screenwriter-relevant industry terms with which you should familiarize yourself:

- Baby writer — The term, which is *not* derogatory, refers to new writers taking their first professional steps in the marketplace.

- Spec script — A screenplay written speculatively, i.e., not on assignment or commissioned.

- Writing sample — Every screenwriter's calling card; a strong spec script that may not sell immediately, but instead will establish its author's skill.

- Paper — Contract

- Ten percenter — Agent or manager

- Call list or call log —The list of calls an industry executive has to make or return.

- Packaged material — Screenplays that have name actors or directors attached to them.

- Elements — The particular name actors or director that bring value to your project.

- Tracking boards — Industry websites dedicated to tracking the performance of spec screenplays introduced by representation to the marketplace.

- The Black List — The industry's most well-regarded and anticipated annual list of unproduced screenplays, published at the end of the year by Franklin Leonard.

- Shooting script — The script that goes before the camera, including scene numbers, the director's input, camera directions, etc.

- Call sheet — An on-set document detailing the material to be shot on a particular day, including locations and elements (actors, props, etc.) necessary.

- Principal photography — The period during which a project is shot.

- Director's cut — The director's assembly of footage shot for a film.

- Final cut — The final assembly of footage shot for a film.

## Getting to Know the Spec Market

When your screenplay is finally ready to be shared, it does not emerge into an unknown world; it seeks to become part of a living, working industry in which scripts are sold and deals are made on a regular basis. Its success or failure will depend largely on what came before it, what is currently being developed, and, just as importantly, the state of the spec market.

### What is the spec market?

The term refers to the virtual industry space in which deals are being made for original creative properties.

Understanding the spec market and how material moves in the industry allows you to get a handle on how your work might perform (execution notwithstanding), simply based on genre identification. While some genres (traditionally thriller, comedy, and action/adventure) tend to move on a more regular basis, others may surface less and represent a greater challenge so far as a sale.

Getting a grasp on what's happening in the marketplace shouldn't dictate what you write next; instead, it should inform you about your script's place in the marketplace, and your best avenue for its success.

### How are spec scripts tracked?

For agents, managers, and development executives there are numerous tracking boards to keep them abreast of developments in the space. For the rest of us? *The Scoggins Report* is where it's at.

*The Scoggins Report*, gathered and published by my good friend Jason Scoggins, onetime lit agent, data geek, and all-around good man, has become the go-to report for tracking what's happening in the industry every month as far as spec and pitch sales are concerned. The free reports, utilized by novices and industry executives alike, provide critical information such as title, logline, genre, writers, and reps for scripts that sold in a given month, as well as information about screenplays that were introduced to the industry by agents and managers during a particular month or year but did not sell.

One of my clients, discussing the market potential of a sci-fi action piece with a development executive, sliced and diced the data provided by *The Scoggins Report* to prove that industry hunger for sci-fi is alive and well.

Sign up for Jason Scoggins' free, twice-a-month and year-end reports at: *https://specscout.com/scogginsreport*.

‐

Now that we've outlined some basic moving-forward expectations, let's start looking at the specifics in your arsenal. First things first: your screenplay.

Chapter Two

# YOUR SCREENPLAY

Congratulations! It's a screenplay. You've read it a hundred times. Tightened and tweaked. Made a fool of yourself reading dialogue out loud as you brought characters to life. It can become anything someday: A summer blockbuster. An Academy Award winner. An indie staple. The sky is the limit.

But first, your newly finished screenplay has a role much more immediate to play: regardless of whether it is ever sold, your screenplay should begin working for you as soon as it's ready. Assuming it displays great writing prowess, a deep understanding of structure, dynamic characters, and compelling word craft, it will open doors, gain interest from the right people, win contests, and generate meetings. It will move your career forward because everyone wants to be associated with good material. Therefore, make sure that before you introduce it to the entertainment industry, it is as good as possible.

Make no mistake: a screenplay should never go out partially or even mostly baked. "Good enough" is nowhere near ready. It has to be as good as you can make it. The competition is too steep, managers and agents too busy, and production and development dollars too few to justify putting anything less than your best out there.

Why, you might ask? As soon as an industry company receives your script, it goes in "the pile." The pile is then assigned to readers, interns, or junior executives, who "cover" the material.

## What is Coverage?

Coverage is the industry-standard document issued to provide executives a quick overview of the script at hand. Coverage includes a logline, short synopsis, comments section, and a "Pass"/"Consider" recommendation.

## Script Recommendations

At the conclusion of each coverage is the coveted recommendation. The recommendation gradient is deeper with some companies than others, but is generally as follows:

- "Pass" — Neither script nor writer warrants consideration at this time.

  ◦ Note: 95% of screenplays receive this recommendation.

- Consider" — There is some merit to the screenplay and/or the writing. The material is worthy of consideration.

  ◦ Roughly 2-3% of screenplays receive this recommendation.

  ◦ Some companies utilize the "Consider with Reservations" recommendation, indicating that while the material is not quite ready, there is something there.

- "Recommend" — Both script and writer are market ready! Read right away.

  ◦ Only 1% of screenplays, at best, receive this recommendation.

## The Coverage File

Once the coverage is completed, your name goes into the company's "coverage file." This may be a simple Excel spreadsheet or a more robust database. Tracked along with your name is your screenplay's title, potentially a logline, and, most importantly, the reader's recommendation. Anytime from here on out when you submit your work to this company, it will be logged in the coverage file, and the person logging will be able to see if the work came from a "Pass" writer, who may than be de-prioritized.

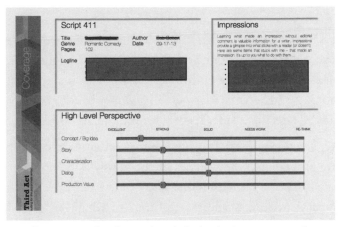

*Actual coverage top sheet from Rob Ripley's The Third Act script consulting service*

### Important to Know:

- Coverages are not shared between companies. They are proprietary.
- Screenplays that receive a "Pass" recommendation rarely get passed on to executives.
- Companies don't share their "Pass" coverage with writers, as it was not written for the writer's benefit.

Because of this, it is of utmost importance that your screenplay is strong, fluid, and focused when you finally send it into the entertainment industry. Its job is to tell your unique story with brilliance, cinematic vision, and economy. It is still likely to garner some "Passes" as is the case with the best scripts, but skill, craft, and professional execution should always be evident.

### Golden Rules for (Almost) Every Screenplay

While this is not a screenwriting book, there are some golden rules for every effective script. Slice and dice them as you will, but it more often than not comes back to this. Of course, exceptions exist. However, if you're a linear storyteller, use the points below as a quick getting-your-script-out-there checklist:

- Strong idea — A screenplay has a greater chance of success when it is built on the foundation of a strong idea. Ask yourself: What is your screenplay about, and what is the idea behind it? A strong idea should be easily outlined. You see it in material from *The Hangover* to *Se7en* to *Moonrise Kingdom*; while the story provides intricate detail, the idea itself is simple and accessible.

- Active protagonist — Nothing annoys executives more than a passive protagonist who watches life helplessly as it happens to him. An effective protagonist is one who is active, like Ben Affleck trying to get American escapees out of Iran, or King George VI aiming to get over a speech impediment so that he may be an effective leader in a time of war.

- Keep the stakes high. — In order for us to care about the story, the stakes for the protagonist have to be high. In order for us to care about your protagonist's journey, what's at stake must be meaningful and detrimental at once; and while not everything has to be life-and-death, it is important that the resolution has a far-reaching impact on your protagonist and his emotional world.

- Believable antagonist — The film industry has blessed us with some fantastic antagonist archetypes: Darth Vader, Joan Crawford in *Mommie Dearest*, Alex Forrest (Glenn Close) in *Fatal Attraction*. Of course, there are much subtler antagonists to think about: the sea itself in *Life of Pi*, not to mention Richard Parker, the tiger; or pretty much any and all adults in *Moonrise Kingdom*. A strong antagonist will stand in the way of your protagonist, hindering needs to be filled and goals to be achieved, all the while being rooted in real motivation and identity.

- Conflict, conflict, conflict — Conflict is at the heart of every good script, be it comedy, horror, suspense, or drama. The fundamentals of conflict are easily boiled down to this: two elements, be they people or things, wanting two different things. An effective conflict will keep your screenplay moving toward a satisfying resolution.

**Useful Tips/Industry Perspective**

Putting together a marketable screenplay is not just about getting the craft right. Here are a few elements industry folks will look for:

- Write characters that actors will want to portray. — Much of getting a movie made these days has to do with attaching the right talent or "elements." In order to attract talent that can get your movie made, write rich, complex, three-dimensional characters.

- Know thy genre and thy audience. — Make the most of your screenplay by understanding where and how your project fits with the current cinematic landscape. While a project can certainly become cross-genre, it's easier to place an exciting screenplay that would readily dictate its own marketing plan. Same goes for TV scripts that have a clear viewer demographic with established, dependable viewing habits.

- Differentiators — The most marketable scripts are different enough to stand on their own and bring something fresh to the game, but similar enough to others that came before to capitalize on a preexisting audience. While this certainly should not dictate your story choices, remember that it could be a consideration for executives. Ask yourself: how does my script add a new point of view or twist to the genre or subject matter?

**Five Screenplay No-Nos**

Now that we talked screenwriting fundamentals, let's talk about what NOT to do from a presentation perspective. The list below outlines some of the most common mistakes writers make, which allow executives to dismiss work before it's even read.

- Don't exceed 120 pages. — Not by even one page. Anytime I bring this up in a seminar, someone asks: What about *Benjamin Button*? *Zero Dark Thirty*? *Titanic*? When you have David Fincher, Kathryn Bigelow, or James Cameron on your side, by all means, go nuts. But until then, as an emerging writer, the onus is on you to remember that the first thing an executive does with any screenplay is check the script's page count. That page number tells the executive this:

- If the screenplay is even one page over 120, the writer implies that he doesn't have to adhere to industry standards, or worse, doesn't know how to write a screenplay that conforms to guidelines and is therefore not a professional.

- The longer the script, the longer the read. An executive has a huge pile of scripts to read on any given day. Of those not recommended by colleagues, he would favor those requiring less time.

- The three-act, 90-120 page format is long tested. Exhibitors have built their screening models around this standard. The longer the screenplay on paper, the longer it will be on film. Exhibitors depend on a set number of screenings per day to hit their numbers. The longer the movie, the fewer the screenings.

• People don't monologue; neither should your characters. — We've all given an impassioned speech in our own imagination to someone who inspired anger, hurt, or even love. But while we all think in big speeches, this is not the realistic way we converse. After confirming an acceptable page count, the executive will flip through the script looking for lots of "chunky" dialogue — a telltale sign of a novice.

• Don't linger! — A good rule of thumb when crafting a scene: start as late as possible, and leave as soon as you can. Every minute shot costs money, so make sure it counts; keep your writing economical and — without cutting the "secret sauce" — be efficient.

• Don't cheat! — ... your font or your margins, that is. Often, in order to cram more content into 120 pages of script, writers change font or cheat margins.

- ◦ Keep your font at 12.

- ◦ Use Courier font.

- ◦ Stay within Final Draft's pagination format.

- ◦ Do not cheat top or bottom margins.

- Leave out camera directions, scene numbers, and wordy descriptions. — Nobody likes an over-embellisher. It's your job to let the reader's imagination take flight. A few surefire ways of stopping this include:

  - ◦ Scene numbers on each scene — those are reserved for the shooting script

  - ◦ Scene direction — Don't PULL INTO A CLOSEUP, PAN ACROSS THE ROOM, or direct your camera to rise, shift, pull in, or pull out. These sorts of directions are for the director to insert, and only interrupt the reading. If you have to, use these camera directions only in service of a critical moment. Otherwise, leave them out.

  - ◦ Over-describing — At this point, the cinematic language is well established. The only time for an elaborate description is when you are introducing something new, significant, or different from what we may have seen before. Keeping your script moving fast with lean action descriptions makes the material more readable.

Your screenplay is your calling card. Don't allow anyone the opportunity to see you for less than what you are: a talented, aspiring professional, who has every possibility of delivering great material.

## Screenplay Adaptations

What better sources are there for rich stories than previously published works?

But before you decide to adapt an old classic or a new favorite to the big screen, be sure to think twice: literary pieces have long provided content for the industry, and many a book's rights are often snatched up before the manuscript hits the general market. Living writers hold the rights to their own material, while older material often has its rights tied up in the writer's estate.

While managers and agents appreciate a good writing sample, a screenplay based on a book whose rights you will likely never get will have a more difficult time making the rounds, as it likely has little potential as a spec — the rights to the material are going to be challenging to get, and the implication is that you may not have your own great ideas on which to base a screenplay.

Only adapt material if you have reason to believe that its rights are readily available. Otherwise, adapt if you know the author, and are able to secure the rights to his material or the subject's life rights. If still you feel compelled to write your screenplay based on source material, adapt older material whose rights are in the public domain, putting an interesting twist on an old favorite.

### Screenplay Feedback — Your Mother Is NOT the Authority You Want (Unless Your Mother Is the Late Nora Ephron)

A screenplay is not a book. It does not exist in its own right. A screenplay is a blueprint. The foundation for a wide collaboration that will engage, inspire, and move many professionals over the years it will take to bring it to screen.

Because of this, it is imperative to get a "second opinion" on your screenplay before you send it into the industry. You need the material to be as tight as possible before you plunge it into the ether.

Nothing will get you a temperature read on your script faster than a seasoned second opinion. Your mother, unless she's the late great Nora Ephron back from the grave or the prolific Callie Khouri, is not the person you want to go to for a good dose of reality. You want to get working within the industry? Time to consider industry friends, consultants, or the all-important industry reader.

### Got Friends?

If you have screenwriting, directing, or producing friends who are working in the industry, this is the time to approach them for their opinion. If you've created a screenwriting community around you, be it a writing group or casually congregating friends, this is the time to utilize it. You are looking for notes, realistic feedback from actual working professionals about the state of your script.

### Screenplay Consultants

Screenplay consultants will work with you on the ongoing development and betterment of your material, in order to bring it to a richer, more professional level. They are numerous and prolific, and many have become industry experts.

Many have published books on the craft of screenwriting; I highly recommend reading through books and materials to find the consultant whose methodology you best connect with. Make no mistake: no two script consultants are the same. Each one has his unique approach, and will look to utilize it to better your work.

While there are many out there, here are the few consultants I regularly recommend:

- Michael Hauge — His clients say that no one understands story better than the no-nonsense Hauge. Michael works regularly with studios and talent on "go projects." He also mentors up-and-coming writers and novelists to help hone their craft, connect character development to structure, and give their scripts the best chance they can have. *www.storymastery.com*

- Pilar Alessandra — As part of her prolific On the Page venture, which offers seminars, classes, and podcasts, the indelible Pilar provides her clientele with detailed evaluations. Pilar is seasoned and personable, with lots of success stories under her belt; her clients swear by her, trust her story instincts, and enjoy working with her. *www.onthepage.tv*

- Jen Grisanti — If you're looking for help developing your spec TV script or original TV pilot, Jen is your girl! A bona fide consultant with teaching gigs at some of television's most renowned fellowship programs, she is a fantastic resource for those looking to develop their television-driven work. *http://jengrisanticonsultancy.com/*

- Ellen Sandler — Writers aiming to break into comedy television writing swear that Ellen is as good as it gets. With years of writing for *Everybody Loves Raymond* to her name, the astute Ellen always pushes her clients further. *http://sandlerink.com*

**Professional Coverage Services**

Coverage services provide writers a temperature gauge from seasoned industry readers, who would potentially encounter your screenplay in a professional environment but, in this context, offer feedback privately and for a fee.

Through coverage services, you are able to submit your screenplay to a professional reader who gauges the reaction your screenplay may garner in a professional setting. The upside? No professional company will see the coverage, and you won't suffer any consequences for submitting material that is not ready.

Professional coverage takes your screenplay out of the solitary world in which it was created, and introduces it to a professional perspective. And while not every reader will love your screenplay, a coverage service should be able to determine whether the material, in broad strokes, succeeds or fails, and make recommendations on how to get it to the next level.

**Warning**: Not all coverage services are created equal. Because good, seasoned readers get paid a certain fee by the industry, they will not read for companies who do not match their regular rates. When choosing a coverage provider, you don't want to err on the side of cheap. Work with the services that offer coverage by seasoned industry readers.

*Recommended Coverage Services*

- ScriptShark — Having run the service for over six years, I hand-picked many of its readers. I remain a believer in its integrity and a fan of the professional readers it has collected.

- ScriptXpert — Final Draft's coverage offering. Run by the devoted Shelly Mellott, the service upholds the highest standards due to Shelly's unrelenting dedication. Shelly would never bring anyone less than qualified to her stable of readers.

- Andrew Hilton/Screenplay Mechanic — One of the readers during my ScriptShark days who came to me via the studios, Andrew now works independently, and is highly valued among screenwriters, including many of my coaching clients. He is a talented reader who cares about his reputation, and his clients swear by him.

- Other Recommended Services:

  ◦ Tracey Becker's Script Swami — When she is not busy producing movies, Tracey provides great screenplay coverage!

  ◦ ScriptGal — The writers who received coverage from her swear by Amanda's determination to go above and beyond!

  ◦ The Third Act — Rob Ripley, a professional movie studio story analyst, now offers his services directly to writers. Rob's approach is constructive, respectful, and challenging; I've sent many a writer to him over the years. You can find his site at *http://thirdactscreenplays.wordpress.com/*.

*Choosing the Coverage Service That's Right for You*

When submitting material for coverage, consider the following:

- Turnaround time — Most services will give you an expectation of turnaround time. If you will not be able to wait calmly for the coverage, consider rushing it for an added fee.

- Choose your reader — If you are going with a company rather than an individual, review the readers' bios, and select the reader whose sensibilities align most closely with yours. In the end, storytelling is a very subjective craft. It serves your purpose to have a reader who responds to similar material as you do.

- Scouting services — This is the added benefit that companies such as ScriptShark and ScriptXpert offer: if your material garners a "Consider" or above through their coverage service, they will introduce it to their industry contacts.

### Receiving, Assessing, and Implementing Script Notes

Everybody hates script notes. Why wouldn't they? After all, script notes remind the writer that your script is not perfect, and that you're still a little ways away from a glorious payday.

No matter how positive or negative the notes, they're there to help elevate your work. Some notes might infuriate you. Others might resonate. Read the notes through, then put them away. Writing and creativity require time to percolate. Take your time figuring out what to do next. And remember:

- When getting coverage, only about 50-60% of the notes you've received will jibe with the story you're trying to tell.

- While all ideas are great in the beginning, you have to try them on to see if they work.

- While a note or a suggestion about a specific scene, moment, or sequence may not resonate, think about the essence of what the analyst was trying to address. The note given may not provide the correct solution, but try to see through to the issues they were trying to resolve.

⤚

Got it? Now that your screenplay has been read, covered, vetted, and analyzed, let's get started on building your career and honing your brand.

Chapter Three

# THE REAL DEAL:
# FEARS, MYTHS, AND RUMORS

Every time I speak at a screenwriting event, I am inundated by relevant questions faced by new and seasoned screenwriters trying to make it. They run the gamut from general rumors and assumptions all the way to fears, as writers confront what lies ahead and what could be working against them as they seek to launch and develop a screenwriting career.

Here, then, are some of the most popular general questions that have come my way over the years.

## Can You Build a Screenwriting Career If You Don't Live in Los Angeles?

Yes.

You don't have to live in Los Angeles to build a screenwriting career, but you should expect to make regular trips to Los Angeles to visit with your contacts, meet development executives, producers, and potential representation on a regular basis.

With Internet and email, a writer can now network from afar, and create all-important opportunities for visibility without a physical presence in Los Angeles. Screenwriting competitions and qualified services that will help get your script out there may become instrumental to your success. To compensate for your location deficiency, make it a habit to produce high-quality new content on a regular basis, giving you a reason to communicate with your growing network regularly. Once representation is secured, you may be asked to travel in for meetings on a regular basis. These travel opportunities will require you to cover cost.

The one thing you won't be able to do when living outside of Los Angeles? Work on a TV show. While you may have the good fortune of getting staffed prior to moving to Los Angeles (though that doesn't happen often), TV writers' rooms demand, unequivocally, all-hands-on-deck. There is simply no way around that.

### Does Moving to Los Angeles Help?

Absolutely. Don't fool yourself into thinking that it won't.

While it certainly is possible to break into the industry remotely, your chances go up once you're in Los Angeles. Not only can you get an industry-driven job and use it to expand your network, here it is much easier to encounter other industry professionals looking for good content. In a city that dances daily to the rhythm of the industry, opportunities abound. Writer-centric events, writing groups, and networking opportunities are everywhere.

Younger writers relocating to Los Angeles may opt to get a job as an assistant or intern, working their way up the ranks, making connections and laying the foundation for their work.

Older scribes may opt to participate in workshops and other events, join a local writing group, or attend industry panels in order to connect with other writers and industry types.

Most importantly, once in Los Angeles, no one will worry about troubling you with the cost of a special trip that might not yield immediate results. Equally, some representation executives prefer taking on local writers, as they are significantly more available for those all-important general meetings, which are scheduled, then cancelled last minute, then scheduled again, at the executives' convenience. Making yourself accessible will allow you to grow your career and network in a consistent fashion.

## What Are the Costs Associated with Building a Screenwriting Career?

At the beginning of each year, I advise clients to budget the upcoming screenwriting year, in anticipation of goals and objectives they set for themselves. While the merit of many offerings and services will be examined in later chapters, the list below includes the variety of services, experts, or initiatives you may choose to budget for:

- Screenplay registration — Each of your screenplays should be registered with the WGA prior to being sent to contests, industry contacts, and executives. Registration can be done online and costs $20 for non-WGA members.

- Screenwriting contests — I recommend entering four to five contests annually. For this, you should budget between $250-$350, depending on the contest.

- Webinars, seminars, and workshops — Cost of attendance can run anywhere from $30 to $500 a pop. If the event in mind allows you to better your craft, gain insight from an expert, or connect with other writers, this may be something you want to pursue, so make sure you budget for it.

- Pitching and listing services — The price point here varies. If you are aiming to engage such a service, plan on spending $200-$500 a year *per screenplay*.

- Coverage and consulting services — The cost of coverage and consultants can vary from $99 to $1,500 (depending whether you go with a service or an expert) per script.

- Screenwriting conferences or events — Conferences are not everyone's cup of tea, and can vary wildly in cost. If you are thinking about making a trip out to, say, the Austin Film Festival or the Great American Pitch Fest in Los Angeles, make sure that you budget not only for entry, but also for housing, expenses, and travel.

- Trips to Los Angeles — A New York–based client recently had his screenplay requested by an LA producer, which was followed by a request for a meeting. The writer not only had to cover airfare, but also housing, car rental, and food.

While these costs may appear steep, remember this: some of them may be deductible, so discuss it with your accountant and see what you may be able to write off. Ultimately, it is up to you what you choose to participate in. Few budget-conscious writers will take on all of these costs in a single year.

### I Am a Mother... Do I Even Have a Chance?

Do you have a great screenplay? If the screenplay has been vetted and the answer is *yes*, then by all means, you have a chance.

That doesn't mean you're not going to have to prove yourself. You will have to convince those you come across that with kids and carpools and PTAs, screenwriting can still be a consistent priority and that you will be able to deliver great material again and again. No one will hire you if they know that they will have to compete with a crying baby to get pages. So be professional. Screenwriting is your job, albeit a highly competitive, initially unpaid one. While you focus on it, leave the diapers and the Neosporin at home.

### Am I Too Old?

Many years ago, when I was teaching a class in Chicago, an older gentleman approached me. Older being the understatement here. He told me he was eighty-four, recently diagnosed with cancer and, following a stroke, given one year to live. He asked me what I thought his chances were for getting representation and building a screenwriting career. Believe me when I tell you that this was one answer I did not want to give.

Alas, I had no choice but to level with him. He was gracious enough to thank me, and even sent me a follow-up email telling me that my honesty was refreshing.

Let's face it: if you're a day over thirty, as far as the industry is concerned, you are no longer young. You have routines. Obligations. Limitations. You will not lie down before an oncoming train for a chance at the spotlight.

But you have strengths, too. Strengths that only come with time:

You had more time to write, to hone your voice.

You are likely to more easily distinguish a good idea from a bad one.

The longer you've lived, the more movie-going hours you've logged. The more TV you've watched. The more books you've read. Play your cards right, and you just might be seen as an expert on a particular genre.

Barring having one foot in the grave, and as long as you've got that great screenplay and some strong, executable ideas to back it up, your age should not be the deciding factor. If you are able to approach your career professionally, to keep up with the pace and expectations of the industry, to churn out great pages and stellar scripts, you make a strong case for your age to not get in the way of your screenwriting career.

## Can Someone Else Do This for Me?

Screenwriting is, without question, an execution-dependent craft. That means that while your idea may be promising, it's what you do with it that's going to count.

If you are not a writer but stumbled upon a single story you want to tell cinematically, by all means, hire the best screenwriter you can get for your buck.

But if it's a prolific, long-lasting screenwriting career you had in mind, better roll back your sleeves and immerse yourself in craft. Careers are built on your ability to deliver great ideas and well-executed screenplays again and again.

Chapter Four

# DEFINING THE WRITER

Whether writing for film, television, or both, no two screenwriters are the same. You may look the same sitting in a writing group or industry event, but — trust me — most writers vary in purpose, intention, and requirements.

Recently, a TV-writing client of mine with a hot TV pilot spec confided in me her frustration about her writing partner: while my client was the one always delivering the great story ideas and intricate plot points, her partner, it seemed, focused his energy on punching up pages and expertly executing dialogue. Though my client realized that she and her partner's skill sets ultimately complemented one other, it spoke to the truth that rarely do two writers possess the same strengths.

## The Prolific Source of Great Ideas

You seemingly pluck great ideas from the universe's prodigious idea repository every day. You see them everywhere, and are able to tell those worth developing from the ones that belong in a virtual trashcan. You not only see ideas; you are able to envision the movies or television shows they will make.

As for the writing itself... that's a different story. You love the moment when an idea clicks or when you "break" a story, and you appreciate the ability to look at the finished work. But the process of writing itself can be a struggle even on the best days.

While your talent for ideas is great, remember that even if a great idea will get you in the room, it's the execution of that great idea that will get you working consistently, and will have agents and managers foaming at the mouth to represent you. Work at your craft to ensure that your ideas are well executed, making you a well-rounded screenwriter, not just an "idea man."

*Tim Robbins in Robert Altman's* The Player *being harassed by the Angry Writer*

## The Writer with One Story to Tell

You have one story to tell, and you've poured blood, sweat, and tears into it. You've taken screenwriting classes. Hired the best consultants. Got a "Consider" coverage. The script might not sit in a popular genre or possess widely popular themes but... Even if it means making it your life's work, you want to see this puppy up on the screen one day.

If this is your one and only cinematic idea, you're not trying to build a screenwriting career; you're trying to get a movie made.

Buckle in and get ready for the long haul. It takes years to get any movie made, and writers pursuing a single project often give years to its realization, occasionally resorting to raising much of the production funds themselves.

Therefore, unless you have that million-dollar script that you're willing to sell and walk away from, you will be of no interest to representation.

Instead, focus on possible production partners, personal resources, or the demanding-but-gratifying do-it-yourself route with crowdsourcing avenues such as Kickstarter. Learn all you can about production and production finance, which will only help in your quest.

### The Reliable Content Creator

You are THAT writer: capable of churning out script after quality script, parlaying solid ideas into promising work. While selling original film or television pilot specs will present as much of a challenge to you as it would anyone else at the outset, you are an ideal candidate for representation. As long as you write consistently and turn in quality work, you will be sent into general meetings, be considered for TV writing staff positions, be brought in to discuss assignments, and, if you're lucky, even land an option or two for your specs.

Keep at it; but don't lose sight of the quality that will become expected of your brand. When working within a genre, ask yourself how your spec is different from previous, similar projects in the space. If you're writing a *Fatal Attraction* for the new millennium, what new twists and elements does your script bring to the table? How does it push this type of film or TV pilot spec further? Keep doing the things that have worked for you in the past, be they writing an extensive outline, going out for coverage, or brainstorming with friends. Ensure the material you are turning in is top-notch, draft after draft. Otherwise, there is always another content creator eagerly waiting to take your place.

### The Assignment Writer

You're a stellar writer but... ideas are not your thing. Relax! All you have to do is produce a few superior specs that will get you attention not only from potential representation, but also production and development executives.

When developing a new project, development and production executives often bring in writers to pitch their "take." Your "take" is the story you would dress the idea up with, your plot and tone contributions to the concept at hand. While the dream often consists of selling your own spec, the reality for today's working screenwriter is that there is a lot of consistency in assignment work. And, lest we forget, writers fortunate enough to get staffed on a TV show spend days, weeks, months, and even years extending and developing someone else's original series concept.

Chapter Five

# KNOW YOUR SEASONS

When is the best time to get your script out? Of course, if you're Dustin Lance Black or John August, industry execs will read your work anytime, anywhere. For the rest of us, here is a broad industry breakdown of what-happens-when as far as submitting screenplays is concerned:

**January – May**

With the holidays firmly behind us, everyone is looking for the next great project, the next great client. While you don't want to send your screenplay or TV script in to agents, managers, or executives (be they old contacts or new introductions) on the first working days of the New Year, this is a good time to get out there. Make sure you avoid the Sundance exodus (during which time many film executives and literary representation executives make their way to Park City) in late January, but short of that... go ahead and get your work out! While a handful of agents and managers will still be busy trying to place a last few pilots into late development, most are reading with vigor, eager to find a new project or client to get excited about.

On the production front, film projects will be shooting year-round. With regular season series (those with a 24-episode pickup) done shooting in March and many midseason replacements shooting through late spring, this is also the time when television pilots are going before the cameras. While some might shoot in earlier months, others may roll just weeks before the pilot delivery date, usually early May.

**May and June**

Upfronts time! The networks have locked their slates, and the next TV season, midseason replacements and all, are announced in mid-May.

Just as quickly as new shows get a green light, many agents and managers start sending out potential pilots for the next pilot season. This will keep going on through October.

While film executives will still be reading material, June is the time of year when most television series start "staffing up," with writers being the first to get staffed. Therefore, agents and managers are not going to be getting to your spec script right away; their top priority is getting their existing clients staffed.

**July and August**

With TV shows starting to film ahead of their season or series premiere, representatives are trying to get the very last available TV writing gigs staffed. The industry goes back to reading at a fairly regular clip. Nonetheless, many executives look for some downtime, enjoying a few weeks vacationing with family or traveling south of the border with friends. In New York, too, executives resort to summer hours, cutting most Fridays down to half days as they head out of the city for fun in the sun. While for many a reading pile will accompany them on their adventures, don't be surprised if response to your material is delayed.

For some executives, the fiscal year will soon come to an end. This is their time to begin trimming development slates, and get ready for new projects in which they want to invest.

**September – November**

As pilot scripts for next season's crop get picked up, spec screenplays are getting read, en masse. Though hardly anyone says it, everyone knows: there's a deadline of sorts ahead. If you still want to get your script out this calendar year, this is the time. Because as soon as November hits... the industry decisively winds down.

## November and December

The holiday season has officially begun, as far as the industry is concerned. Sure, many will still be working through mid-December, but most will be busy with holiday shopping, making important company decisions, and tying up the year's remaining loose ends. If the collective "they" will be reading anything, it's the past year's scripts that made it to The Black List, which usually gets announced in mid-December. Any scripts on the executive's virtual desk that haven't been read yet will likely languish in a pile, and be forgotten when the new crop of scripts arrive come January.

Unless you are a hot writer coming out with a highly anticipated spec, during this time you're best advised not to submit anywhere. Instead, send holiday cards to executives who acknowledged your writing along the way, perfect an existing screenplay, or start on new work, preparing for January when you can start submitting your work again.

Chapter Six

# MANAGING EXPECTATIONS: WHEN THINGS SHIFT, CHANGE, OR PLAIN DON'T GO YOUR WAY

If you've been at this screenwriting thing for any amount of time, chances are there have been changes in your trajectory, shifts in direction, disappointments, and hurdles.

### A Previous Screenplay Did Not Gain Any Traction

You wrote it. You loved it. You were convinced it was The One. You reached out to industry contacts, posted the material on a listing service, entered contests, used online introduction services, even had a few industry folks take a look at the work but... nothing. Crickers. So... what's next?

You've got two options:

- Go back to the beginning. — Figure out what didn't work. Don't make excuses — the problem is with the work. Send the screenplay to people who can punch holes in it if you haven't done it already, get as many scathing reviews as you can. It may be painful, but it will help you understand what didn't work. Find the comments that resonate and improve the story you're trying to tell, then spend time executing them in the best possible way.

- Move on and don't look back. — Sometimes it's just as important to know when to let a script go as it is to know how to improve the work. Don't get trapped in years of rewrites that will keep you from moving on to your next, and potentially better, work. That said, be sure to look back and identify why it didn't receive the traction you thought it would. Was it in the subject matter? Genre? Execution? Moving forward, you want to improve on your last work and not repeat the same mistakes.

### You Are Part of a Writing Partnership

Every partnership wants to end up like Rossio and Elliott. Prolific. Talented. Seemingly harmonious. Financially well off. The destination you are looking for is established by actions. At its outset, however, questions about the potential and stability of the writing team will be everywhere, even if they are not voiced.

- Make sure you have a strong relationship with the person you're working with. — You don't have to be best friends; this is a business partnership and you should set rules and expectations for it accordingly. If needed, put together a mutually agreed upon contract to clarify the parameters of the partnership.

- Ask yourself: Why is this person the right writing partner for me? — What does this person bring to the table that I don't? How do we complement one another? The people you and your writing partner will come in contact with will look to see if there are any cracks in the partnership before they commit to working with you.

- Writing partnerships often trigger this question: Who is the REAL writer here? — Once again, make sure the roles within the partnership are clear, and both partners are comfortable with the distribution of the work.

**You Are Coming Out of a Writing Partnership**

As with any divorce, coming out of a writing partnership can be messy. The further you are in your career, the more challenging it will be to walk away gracefully. Though most would hope that your partnership ends cordially, the reality is that, if they didn't end badly, most partnerships wouldn't end.

Here are a few things to pay heed to as you're walking away:

- Agree on distribution of assets. — If this is a case of writing separately but sharing credit on all completed material for the sake of the partnership, the writers may agree to divide the assets based on who did the heavy lifting and where. In other scenarios, both writers may feel equal ownership of the work, in which case the script or scripts in question would not be available for you to show as your own.

- If you are represented as a team, have conversations with your representation about representing you individually.

- As far as your network goes, which thus far knew you as part of a team, your next script is a must-ace. — Everyone will be looking to see if you've lost some of your mojo walking away. Be sure to cover all of your bases before you submit again professionally.

- Be clear about the brand you want to develop for yourself. — You will have to reestablish yourself as an individual writer, so be sure you do so with purpose.

- Take the high road, always. — Your writing partner might have been certifiable, but he must've also brought good things to the partnership. Be respectful when discussing the partnership. That respect will go a long way.

## You've Had Success Before, and Are Now Trying to Build Momentum Again

If you've had success some years back, but have since not written or sold a new screenplay, you might want to get cracking on new work. The industry looks to see momentum build for a writer whose material and brand is getting interest, not a stoppage to the professional-grade work.

This doesn't mean you can't build momentum up again. Reintroduce yourself by reminding executives and representation that you sold a script, won a contest, or wrote a screenplay that generated a lot of buzz. Without fudging facts, position yourself in the best light.

The best thing to do to curtail any concerns about the ebbs and flows of your writing habits is to put your head down and do the work. The only thing that is entirely undeniable in this industry is exceptional content. Work not only on your next script, but also on the ideas you want to develop. Convince the industry that you are ready to be a player again by coming forth with focused, brand-extending content that is sure to put you right back on the map.

## Representation Dropped You

It's disappointing, but there's little you can do now but pick yourself up and dust yourself off. In the long run, this will be a good thing. Your representation dropped you because they felt they couldn't effectively develop your brand or sell your work. Being dropped is the perfect motivator to find an agent or manager who can.

You may feel embarrassed. What does being dropped say about you? The truth is that it happens to writers every day, and many recover from it. The important thing is to explore whether the representation who dropped you is willing to elaborate as to why, which will illuminate a few things you might need to do differently next time.

Finding new representation to work with should not be as difficult as it was the first time around, assuming you first secured representation based on strong work. Simply let new potential representation know that you were previously with XYZ Management, and, if the firm is of any merit, just by sheer association they may show interest.

## Interest Does Not Develop into Success

You've gotten some interest, but even though a number of production companies were enthusiastic about your script, their interest did not develop into any sort of tangible success, i.e., a script option or script sale.

While this is disappointing, don't overlook the positives that have emerged: you made yourself an industry fan! Make sure to thank those you were talking to for their interest, and lay the groundwork for sending them the next script you have. Just because it didn't work out this time, doesn't mean that next time you will suffer the same fate!

## A Script Sale Did Not Result in a Produced Movie

You got so excited. You told everyone you know. This is it! You made it! And then... crickets. The script never made it off the shelf. Now everyone's asking: What happened to your movie? When's it coming out?

Congratulations! You are now officially part of the club. Most working screenwriters out there have sold screenplays that have never made it onto the screen. Think of it as a right of passage.

A failed TV script may just prove to put your career on track. A script sale in TV land, whether or not resulting in a produced show, puts you in an elite category. Writer Noah Hawley contributed a column to *The Hollywood Reporter* about just this topic ("Why a Failed Pilot Actually Means Success," March 2013), noting that TV writers traditionally fail up, with every failure serving as a stepping-stone and a validation toward your next opportunity.

Chapter Seven

# SIMPLE THOUGHTS FOR TOUGH TIMES

My client Kelly once wrote to me:

*"I had to face my writer's panic that I might never make it, and that led me to realize (and this is huge for my fellow writers, too) that I cannot envision myself achieving the goal. Meaning, I have no idea what it will be like, taste like, smell like to get a manager and sell a script. Imagining that moment in detail (I call this Goal Porn) is a huge part of my daily process to keep me motivated and passionate about the script."*

Building a screenwriting career is not easy. But just because it's not easy, doesn't mean it's not achievable. The longer you stay in this game, the more your chances for success will increase. As the great Michael Hauge once told me, this is a game of tenacity. Keep writing, and you will get there. The sooner you know this, the better off you will be: building a screenwriting career is about you the writer rather than about any one script. It is a marathon. It is hardly ever, even in the best cases, a sprint.

Just like everyone else, marathon runners have been known to get discouraged at times — their time is too slow, they struggle at a certain leg of the race. Building a screenwriting career can be very much the same. Try to anticipate what will push you through the tough moments while you're still feeling motivated, not when you're down and without any semblance of confidence. Put ideas, sayings, motivators on your corkboard, in a desk drawer, or in a computer file to help you get through those tough days, when a screenplay did not sell, when you failed to win a high-value contest, or when you went out with what you thought was a great script, but received no interest. This has happened to every writer working out there. But to get through it, you have to stay tenacious.

Remember, the thing that will get you through the toughest moments is your love of the work. Therefore, protect your passion for writing as though it was an asset. Keep writing, creating, and mulling over ideas, and remember that even when things are difficult in the business world, it's in the writing that you will find yourself again and again. And if you need a moment? A little space? Give yourself a break. In time, your passion will bring you to the computer again and again.

Find your team, those who will get you through the tough moments, who will allow you to take a step back, grab a bit of distance, then find your passion again. When those don't work? Follow my client Don's lead, and watch underdog movies back to back: *Rocky*, *Rudy*, *Cinderella Man*. He throws in *The Karate Kid* and *Remember the Titans* on particularly bad days. But every time, these movies get him back to what inspired him to be a screenwriter in the first place.

Remember this: rejection is part of the game. If you haven't gotten rejected, you aren't doing right by your screenplay. Send it to as many people as you can, and expect that for most it will likely be a pass. Even today's working writers were once not immune to rejection — it's the reality of getting your screenplay out there. The more you get your script out there, the more rejections you will get. But building a screenwriting career is not about those necessary but disappointing NO's. It's about getting that life-changing YES.

The bottom line? Prepare for the tough moments with as much focus as you prepare for success. Hurdles are part of the road any achievement-driven aspirant is going to take. Whether you have a friend to turn to, a writing group, a career coach, or a movie that will pull you through it again and again, it's important that you prepare yourself for the tough moments as well as your success. Your career may just depend on it.

Chapter Eight

# INDUSTRY NEWS, BLOGS, SCREENPLAYS, AND WEBSITES

This is it. You got your coverage, you read up on the spec market, you know your seasons... you are ready to go. Success or bust! But making a go of a screenwriting career requires more than just the right script. You have to develop a comprehensive understanding of the industry you are trying to penetrate. Everyone says that luck has something to do with it. But luck has also been known to favor the prepared.

## Industry News

When I told my friend manager/producer Dallas Sonnier of Caliber Media that I was writing this book, he said, "Tell writers that the most important thing they can do is read industry news. Regularly." For the record, Dallas put his money where his mouth is: he started subscribing to *The Hollywood Reporter* when he was a thirteen-year-old kid.

I am a big believer in each writer being the champion of his own career, arming himself with as much industry knowledge as he can. While later in your career an agent or a manager may suggest that you lay off the trades so that you don't end up subconsciously chasing the trends, until such time as you have a pro picking and choosing which information you are fed, it is up to you to stay on top of as much information as you can. And while you don't have to know every company with a studio deal out there, it is in your best interest to keep abreast of what's happening in the entertainment universe.

The best tool invented for anyone not too eager to troll for industry news every day? Email notifications. Sign up, and industry news will find its way back to your desktop, laptop, smartphone, or tablet.

- *Deadline.com* — The industry's go-to news blog, it offers news stories reported as they happen. The site offers free content and breaking news alerts

- *StudioSystemNews.com* — A powerful news aggregate offering twice-daily news roundups from over a hundred relevant sources as well as specialized newsletters.

- *The Hollywood Reporter* — Offers weekly print editions (forty-eight comprehensive issues) and daily PDFs for a monthly or annual subscription fee.

## Industry Databases

If knowledge is power then entertainment industry databases are the batteries powering your smarts. Here is a quick overview of where industry pros get their data:

- The Studio System — This industry database, which can be found at every major studio, representation, and production company, is far more expensive than what most writers out there can afford.

- IMDbPro —The pro arm of the fan-driven IMDb, this site has come a long way in a short time. Actors thrive here as they are able to upload headshots and résumés, while many an industry executive utilize their highly affordable and confirmed-enough data.

- ItsOnTheGrid — Specializes in development and spec information, including open writing assignments and projects in development. While it is not as comprehensive as the previous databases mentioned, it does focus on a high-value sector of information.

## Online Writing Communities

The Internet allows writers from different countries, walks of life, and experience levels to come together to share information, do research, and ask pertinent questions. Below is a list of popular online destinations:

- Script Magazine — The industry staple is now alive and well on the Web. Find fantastic feature articles, expert blogs, and other writing-relevant content at this popular destination for screenwriters.

- DoneDealPro —Possibly the Internet's single most popular screenwriters' forum, here you will find answers to most any burning screenwriting question, be it business or craft oriented.

- ScriptWriters Network — A nonprofit organization formed in the late '80s, the network offers events, education, and useful links, to name a few.

- International Screenwriters' Association — This comprehensive group offers resources, classes, events, articles, and even writing gig opportunities through its robust website.

- Stage 32 — A social networking site for film, television, and stage creatives, inviting you to build your network, list your projects, and find work. The fast-growing site offers extensive discussion forums, online webinars and events, and a great platform through which creatives can connect.

## Podcasts, Bloggers, and Other Community Members

There is endless content on the Internet, just waiting to be devoured. But how do you decide which to prioritize? Here is a list of some of the more consistent and popular blogs and podcasts:

- OnThePage — Pilar Alessandra's podcast has become an industry staple. Offering interviews with everyone from screenwriting experts to working professionals, its free downloads are popular among aspiring and working writers.

- John August and Craig Mazin's ScriptNotes — Podcast from two working super-screenwriters, with lots of fantastic insights into the world of a working scribe.

- GoodInARoom — On *http://goodinaroom.com,* pitching expert Stephanie Palmer offers valuable insight and guidance in her blog.

- Go Into The Story by Scott Myers — Recently integrated with The Black List, Scott's blog is prolific and expansive. A produced screenwriter, WGA member, and screenwriting professor, Scott offers fantastic insight and commentary on recent industry developments.

- The Business — KCRW's weekly show led by *The Hollywood Reporter*'s Kim Masters explores recent headlines and delivers in-depth interviews and feature stories. Available for download.

- The Bitter Script Reader — The name says it all. This bitter script reader has no desire to see writers make the same mistakes over and over again!

Additional notable blogs and bloggers include: Ted Hope's Hope for Film, Ken Levine, Broken Projector with Scott Beggs and Geoff LaTulippe, BambooKillers, Notes from a Hack, Complications Ensue, and many more!

## Other Websites You Might Find Useful

There are endless websites out there that help writers, provide insight, and extend the community. While I can't list all of them (my apologies to those who are not included), here are a few more worth taking a look at:

- ScriptShadow (*http://scriptshadow.net*) — A polarizing site that has as many fans as it has critics, Carson Reeves' review site provides aspiring screenwriters with invaluable input.

- WordPlay (*http://wordplayer.com*) — A highly educational site loaded with screenwriting-centric articles written by working screenwriters.

- Collider (*http://collider.com*) — More industry news, reviews, and interviews!

- Film School Rejects (*www.filmschoolrejects.com*) — News, trailers, and distinct points of view!

### Screenwriting and the Twitterverse

For many of today's writers, the conversation begins in the Twitterverse. Not only does the platform allow writers to connect with others and exchange meaningful information in 140 characters or less, it also allows novices to connect with working professionals.

The concern? Learning to filter the noise that comes at you through the Twitter ether. What you should do with your script and what you should write about next are only a small portion of the opinions and information Twitter brings your way every day. So be sure to deploy deliberate filters and conviction in your own path before you engage. Not sure how to do that? Put an informed strategy in place, i.e., identify the idea/s that are most strategic to your brand, that extend what you've done well in the past, put your core competencies on display, and allow you new opportunities to expand your established voice, and don't divert from those, despite the tweets that come your way.

Also facilitated by the Twitterverse: ScriptChat (*scriptchat.blgospot. com*) and TVWriterChat (*tvwriterchat.com*). Now TweetChatting on two continents, both groups offer weekly tweetchats with a variety of experts, from screenwriters to working professionals, gurus to folks of the craft.

Twitter is also a great way to stay on top of what's happening: *Deadline.com*, *Script* Magazine, and many others are tweeting breaking news and other pertinent information to followers.

If you're not on Twitter yet, create your profile and start building lists of Following and Followers. Search by the most relevant hashtags (#screenwriting, #scriptchat, #amwriting, etc.), and use this ever-popular site to expand your horizons and your network.

### Other Screenplays

Just as important as seeing movies and becoming familiar with the trends of the industry is becoming familiar with other screenplays that are creating buzz and getting produced out there.

Here are some of the most popular sites for finding trending, just-produced or just-released material:

- SimplyScripts — Offers PDFs for produced and unproduced screenplays, as well as TV scripts, Academy Award–nominated screenplays, and much more.

- Drew's Script-O-Rama — This campy site, with full commentary delivered since 1995, has been lauded by *Entertainment Weekly*.

- Awesome Films — Screenplays for classic films, both old and new, available for a fee.

- *IMSDb.com* — Repository of screenplays for movies that were recently released, but you do have to read online.

- *ReadWatchWrite.com* — Brad Johnson shares one notable script every Monday as part of his Monday Script Share.

### Your Local Screenwriting Network

In this day and age, there are screenwriters, and therefore screenwriting groups, most everywhere. While writing can keep you in solitude, screenwriting groups and networks can get you out of your cave, connect you with like minds, and keep you engaged in the all-important screen-writing conversation.

To get you started, here are a few examples of active local groups:

- Chicago Screenwriters Network — Founded in 1995, the CSN works hard to connect Windy City writers with the working in-dustry, putting on screenwriting-driven events, conducting an annual contest, and bringing in relevant speakers.

- Northwest Screenwriters Guild — Founded in 1997, this orga-nization is entirely volunteer based, and is known for not only cultivating its members, but also bringing in relevant speakers from Los Angeles for pitch events and focused workshops.

- NYC Screenwriters Collective — In existence for many years and formerly NYC Screenwriter Meetup, this group has members that number in the thousands and offers script reviews, craft tutorials, and much more.

- Dallas Screenwriting Association — Founded in 1989, this is one of the oldest screenwriting groups in the States, with a broad, established audience. This group brings in fantastic guest speakers and also does monthly scene reads.

Can't find a screenwriting network or group in your neck of the woods? Screenwriters are everywhere, so get industrious and start your own group! Building a strong writers' community will help you not only gain new valuable insights, but also provide you with a safe venue for developing your work, which will surely strengthen your writing.

Chapter Nine

# CREATING A FOCUSED
# CAREER STRATEGY

Among its many definitions, the *Merriam-Webster Dictionary* defines *strategy* as:

> "*A careful plan or method; the art of devising or employing plans or stratagems towards a goal.*"

Many writers have a tendency to try anything and everything they hear about (without any particular rhyme or reason) in the hopes of moving their screenwriting career forward; the good old strategy of throwing everything at the wall and seeing what sticks. Others prefer to keep their heads down and stay in the comfort zone that is their writing space. Me? I prefer approaching one's career with knowledge, focus, and purpose.

## Defining Long-Term Aspirations

Within the construct of building a screenwriting career, an aspiration should be the thing that you're working toward.

In the context of this book, let's rely on the following definition of aspirations:

> "*Strong desire, longing or aim; Ambition.*"

One aspires to win an Oscar. To become a staff writer. To write the next blockbuster summer comedy. Your long-term aspirations should look to the final destination. But if you want to start building an executable action plan for your screenwriting career... the time has come to talk short-term goals.

## Setting Short-Term Achievable Goals for Screenwriting Success

A client once emailed me: "I set my annual goal! I am going to get my screenplay optioned!"

If only it were that easy.

When setting a script option as her short-term, achievable goal, my client, despite her best intentions, inevitably set herself up for failure.

Your screenwriting career goals should be short-term objectives, ones that fall within your control. In that spirit, humor me one more time as I turn to *Dictionary.com*:

*"Goal: The result or achievement toward which effort is directed."*

No matter how much effort one might put toward getting her screenplay optioned, whether or not my client's goal is actually achieved falls entirely outside of her control. She has no power over industry trends, company funds, executives losing their jobs, all of which could get in the way of achieving her goal. The same would be said if she set her goal as winning an Oscar or writing the highest-grossing summer action movie. These are all aspirations; desired results that you have little to no control over.

Career goals should be comprised of actionable opportunities within your control that will hopefully bring your aspiration closer to coming true. Your objective, then, is to identify actionable goals that you can pursue, ones that will fuel your journey and fill up the tank of your career as it gains speed and goes flying down the road.

## Becoming an Expert: Your Brand

If you've been contemplating your screenwriting career for any length of time, I'm sure you've heard plenty of talk about becoming an expert or establishing your brand. Becoming an expert means mastering a single genre, and writing multiple scripts within it, be they feature film or TV in format, thereby comprising your brand. This allows not only for your voice and brand to be clear and solid, but also for your representation to understand how they are going to market you. While this approach seems limiting to some, trust me when I tell you that it is the most solid bet you can make as far as a long-term career is concerned.

When you're trying to break in, nothing is more important than your potential representation understanding what sort of writer you are. This is how they will know which production companies and executives your skill set and talent might be right for, and how to begin to consistently and effectively build your fan base. At the start of your career, your brand and expertise is the best weapon you've got. Settle on a genre you can excel in, and dedicate yourself to creating multiple works within it. Know that though you will not be confined to this genre for the entirety of your career, it will be where, if you're lucky, you will make your start.

Don't believe me? Let's look at a few current examples from working professionals. Adam Cooper and Bill Collage (writing team) had their first comedy script produced in 2003. Since then, they've gone on to write other comedies, such as *Accepted* and *Tower Heist*. But even though they started in comedy, they are now venturing out. At the time of this writing, they are developing a historical drama, *Exodus*, with Ridley Scott, and an HBO project (this one a holiday drama) with Ron Howard. Want another? John Spaihts broke into the industry in 2007 on the merit of his sci-fi script *Shadow 19*. Since then, he sold a number of sci-fi scripts, sealing his status as the industry's sci-fi go-to guy with *Prometheus*.

The industry has shifted aggressively in the last decade. Expectations put on a screenwriter have shifted as well, from authoring a single screenplay that could sell to becoming an ongoing reliable source for creativity and content. Due to the rise in competition and decline in box office receipts and consequent spec sales, a screenwriter has to approach his career with a deliberate plan. A manager friend recently confided in me that these days it takes twice as long as it did five years ago to sell a spec script. Because of this, agents and managers prefer to work hard developing talent that will produce winning material again and again, reaping the rewards from time invested for years to come.

Becoming an expert makes you not only a seasoned and trusted source of content, but also the writer executives will want to work with.

Study films similar to the screenplays you have under your belt, and contemplate when they were released, and what was their chosen, conventional or unconventional, release path. Remember, Hollywood is rarely looking to reinvent its ways, but rather prefers to repeat its tried-and-true successes. While knowing all about release paths is not in your job description, you will establish yourself as a professional if you are able to talk knowledgably about the general expectations set for the type of projects you have at hand.

## Championing Your Screenplay

From conception to realization, your role as a screenwriter will change at different junctures of your project's life cycle.

At first, you are the screenplay's one and only champion. The only person for whom it exists, and who has undying faith in what it can be one day.

Then people get involved. Agents or managers might make suggestions for rewrites before they take the material to the industry. With any luck, producers and development executives will get involved and look to further alter the material. And that is only the beginning.

As material gains momentum, more people get involved. A director will bring his own vision, which you will be requested to incorporate into the script. If a different direction is desired, a second or third writer may be brought on board.

Filmmaking is nothing if not a collaborative process. And within it, you will have to understand and inevitably accept where you fit in. As a storyteller, it's your role to champion the story you're telling, but that, too, comes with boundaries.

Film is a director's medium. The final product is not one you read on the page, but one you see on the screen. Because of this, many writers will have to relinquish control, and defer to the captain of the ship to make the best cinematic product collaboratively.

While you may fight to protect your script, to keep the material produced closest to your original vision, you will likely not be included in producorial or directorial decisions. At least at the outset of your career, don't expect to be given a producorial position as anything more than a symbolic "gimme." Unless you're working on a super-low budget where you will be wearing every hat you could possibly get, producorial decisions will, inevitably, be above your pay grade.

Trying to insert yourself into roles you have not earned will do little to promote your career, earn good will, or keep you as an integral part of the team. Let others do what they do well, and understand your role in the realization of the project while respecting what others bring. An old writing client once insisted on receiving a producer's credit when his first screenplay was getting some heat. To win a bidding war, the production company gave it to him. But when this writer insisted on having a vote on decisions he had no experience to make and thereby made the process painful and cumbersome for everyone involved, the writer was quickly dropped, and the production company brought in a known talent to finish rewrites.

### Today's Genre Popularity

In today's industry landscape, no two genres get the exact same reception. This has been true for many years, and remains so today. It comes down to this: if you have two screenplays that are well written, polished, with effective conflict and compelling characters, it's the one that falls within the more popular genre that will have a better likelihood of selling, or getting its writer the attention he deserves.

Here is roughly how screenplays have ranked according to genre in recent years, from most popular to least:

- Thriller — Year over year, thrillers prove to be strong sellers. Within this genre fall political thrillers, psychological thrillers, action thrillers, and budget-friendly contained thrillers.

- Comedy — Often affordable to make for lack of expensive special effects and popular with the powerful 18–24 year-old male audience, comedies include dark comedies and romantic comedies, though romcoms do tend to be heavily cast/director dependent.

- Action/Adventure — Action adventures may incorporate a variety of subgenres, including comedy, sci-fi, or thriller. While they are traditionally expensive to make, they can also make or break a studio's summer in the box office, or elevate a production company to a powerful player.

- Sci-Fi — Another genre that is not cheap to make, but highly popular when built on the shoulders of powerful story and exciting innovations. This is the genre in which the industry's old adage of "different but same" is probably most prevalent.

- Horror — Ever popular with the younger generation of moviegoers out for cheap thrills without demanding much production value or sophistication, horror screenplays, when done right and offering new scares, still see some sales.

- Drama — While drama, by definition, is at the core of every cinematic story, straight drama scripts remain some of the more challenging to place. Their slow pace and intricate character work often struggle to win over the younger sectors. Within this genre fall such subcategories as family dramas, period dramas, medical dramas, political dramas, and social dramas. Ones that are executed effectively may see sales, and help their writer secure representation.

Chapter Ten

# LAUNCHING YOUR
# SCREENWRITING CAREER

There's more than one way to skin a cat, and certainly more than one way to jump-start a screenwriting career. While your path may include any of the options below, a winning combination, or a route entirely your own, here are some of the more popular ways for writers to get your screenwriting the sort of attention that will help move your careers forward.

## Securing Representation

Everyone wants representation, but only a small percentage of screenwriters trying to break in are ready for it. When representing a client, agents and managers help their writers get "out there" by putting their client's screenplays in the right hands. Agents focus on the sale, on booking you into open writing assignments, or getting you on a TV writing staff (which usually can only happen once you've sold a screenplay or generated serious buzz); managers will not only introduce your material to executives of worth, but will also — in the best-case scenarios — help you develop material that meets the needs of the marketplace.

It's important to remember that having representation will not guarantee your success. Representation will offer you a strong advocate in the industry, one who, with any luck, is considered a trusted source for good writers and strong material. That said, you will also have to keep feeding them the sort of high-quality, honed material they can easily get behind.

If you sign with representation, remember that this is not the final destination of your journey. In many ways, this is where the hard work begins. Your representation will expect you to perform, continuously and on a high level. If you sit on your laurels or expect them to do all the work, there is always another talented, ambitious, hardworking writer eager to take your place.

To learn more about securing representation and becoming the sort of writer agents and managers want to work with, turn to Chapter 19.

## Getting Attention Through Contests and Pitch Events

Over the years, I've had the good fortune of observing many a writer whose road to success started with a contest win or a winning turn at a pitch event. These avenues offer significant opportunities for exposure and network growth, though they do require a financial investment.

### Screenwriting Contests

Perhaps the most well-known contest win is that of Mike Rich, who became a Nicholl Fellow with *Finding Forrester* in 1998. This win stands above the rest simply because the winning screenplay went on to be produced with a hot director and a talented cast. However, while this example certainly puts on display the best-case scenario of what can come of winning a screenwriting contest, it is important to remember that such stories are few and far between.

Screenwriting contests can be instrumental for getting your name and your work out there. Agents, managers, producers, and development executives certainly pay attention to those who win or place in the final rounds of the most reputable contests, often eager to review the work and see if the writer could be a fit for them.

Turn to Chapter 15 to learn more about the most relevant screenwriting contests out there.

*Pitch Events*

As you will read in Chapter 18, the reality is that no one sells a script at a pitch event. Over the years, writers' expectations have inflated, causing many to miss the point of attending such an event: making those all-important industry connections. While participation in such events does not come cheap, it is a great way to get in front of executives, agents, and managers appropriate for yourself and your work. While I never recommend putting all your eggs in one basket, I know many a writer whose career efforts are invested exclusively in such events.

The danger of which one must be aware is that it's all too easy to become a professional event participant, rather than a professional screenwriter. If you've gone to a number of such events but have not been able to create meaningful connections that lead to requests for your work, it might be time to reconsider the material at hand, or explore other avenues for getting yourself and your work out there. The bottom line? If you have market-ready material and honed your pitch, and you do pitch fests right, you should only have to attend them once or twice before you see your career take flight.

For more about pitch events, Chapter 18 is where it's at.

## Working Your Way Up

For many a young writer, the best way to break in is to work your way up. Come to Los Angeles, get a low-level job at a production company or representation firm, work crazy hours, then make your way up, forging all-important contacts, building your network, and learning from the inside how the industry works. Many executives expect young writers trying to break in to pursue this path. It is, without a doubt, the path of hard work, but if you're good at your job and do it right, impress the right people and never give up, your hard work will earn you those stripes.

More importantly, and though it might take years, you will never position yourself better for success than you will once you are on the inside. When working within the industry, you will be reading material and getting to know industry folks on a regular basis. There is no telling how far any given industry relationship will take you.

That said, there is, as with everything, a downside: jobs with production companies, on movie sets, or with representation companies are not easy to come by, nor do they pay very well. You will be expected to put in long, LONG hours, leaving little time for your creative efforts. Every job opening inspires steep competition. Expect to go on many a job interview before you land one.

This path, logical though it might seem, is not right for everyone. It is for the young, those able to live on limited income and willing to put in long hours year after year while making significant sacrifices. For those further along in their lives, with kids, a certain standard of living you're used to or specific financial requirements, this is likely NOT the path.

### Networking to Success

Remember *Field of Dreams*? "If you build it, he will come?" Well, this, or a version of this memorable line, could be said for building a powerful industry network. If you build it, they will show up when you have good work to share.

Networking is something you should be doing on an ongoing basis. Marketing yourself to industry executives regularly will certainly raise your chances for success.

- Good content moves — For many writers, the challenge is getting good content in the right hands. If what you write shows real industry promise, the people in your network (assuming they are connected) will pass the work on to others if it's not right for them.

- Your network = Your fans — If you deliver solid work again and again, your network will become littered with fans, who in turn will become your advocates.

- Possibilities — While your material may not be exactly what one of your contacts is looking for, if your voice falls within their sweet spot, don't be surprised if they approach you with an idea for a project to develop.

## Self-Financing

If you have the means or the connections... why not self-finance? Getting a visionary up-and-coming director, putting together a stellar crew, and turning your screenplay into a movie worthy of Sundance is the fastest way to get your name out there.

But money is not everything, and it's important to remember that. With your own money, or that of relatives and friends, it's that much more important to make sure that the screenplay is beyond reproach, giving the movie the best chance you can.

If you do choose to go this route and self-finance, one thing's for sure: a lot of begging will come into play. You will have to ask friends and associates to step up to the plate and help you turn this crazy endeavor into a success. And when things shift, change, or go south, you will have to answer to them.

A word to the wise: never take a second mortgage out on your house to finance your movie. Never take anyone's retirement money or life savings. No movie out there is worth that. It may be your dream, but when all is said and done, a movie is what you will have. So raise your funds the old-fashioned way: from family, and from wealthy friends who have a little extra they want to invest to help get your screenwriting career underway. Kickstarter and similar online platforms are also avenues for raising cash. Still, know that you will have no guarantee that once the movie is done you will gain representation or break even financially. It is not guaranteed that you will have a movie that cuts together, which is why you want to bring on board the most seasoned crew you can attract. Ultimately, having a movie of your work produced will certainly push you forward a significant step.

That said, it's important to remember that this is not the right path for everyone out there. In fact, it's a path that only few should and can take. Investing your own money, or money that you've solicited, will inevitably involve you in production and make you that much more accountable for the film's fate. If it all goes south, it's not some faceless corporation that will be losing its shirt.

### Breaking into Television

Today's TV writer must be ambitious, determined, and consistent. After all, there is no easy path into TV. You will likely utilize many of the elements noted earlier in this chapter. Additionally, here are some popular ways to break into television in today's market:

- Receive a TV fellowship. — Six networks award fellowships to qualifying writers aspiring to break into television. Those networks are: NBC/Universal, CBS, WB, Fox, Nickelodeon, and Disney/ABC. Each program is different; some offer a limited weekly pay, while others allow writers to observe various writers' rooms. Requirements are different from fellowship to fellowship; each comes with its unique deadlines, and some are diversity based. In all, fewer than fifty fellowships are awarded annually, but they bring a lot of worthwhile recognition and are a great way to connect with television writers and executives.

- Become a writers' assistant. — Put in a few years as a writers' assistant and... the sky's the limit! With any luck and a little time, you might just be invited to contribute to an episode. If that goes well, making it into the writers' room is not unheard of.

- Work your spec. — Did you know that TV shows with a season order of twenty-two episodes or above are obligated to get an episode (or two) from a "freelance" writer on air? While the freelancers hired are often "friends and family" or established writers who left the writers' room at the end of a previous season, a fantastic TV spec, if written for the appropriate show, is a great way to get yourself noticed.

- Find new avenues to get your voice heard. — From essay readings to sketch events, writers have found new, interesting ways to get their voices heard, garner attention, and ultimately get staffed!

Chapter Eleven

# YOUR BODY OF WORK:
# MATERIALS ALL WRITERS SHOULD
# HAVE IN THEIR ARSENAL

Embarking on a screenwriting career should not happen on a whim. In order to be taken seriously by the various executives you will come across from the very early stages of your journey, here is an overview of materials you should have ready to share.

## Current Screenplays

Jason Scoggins, who, prior to *The Scoggins Report* made his name in the representation game, once told me that when he was a ten percenter, he wouldn't consider taking a screenwriter on unless said screenwriter came complete with two polished similar-genre screenplays. While not every agent and manager adheres to this approach, it's a worthwhile guideline for which you can prepare.

Now, when we're talking completed screenplays, we mean screenplays for which notes have been received, for which you've done the necessary rewrites, and which have gone through a final polish. Completed, in industry terms, means that the screenplay is, beyond reprieve, ready to show.

Whether you've got one, two, or five scripts ready, current screenplays should be ones you've completed recently, not ten years ago. If you sent your screenplay out ten years ago and it got no positive response, it's time to put it behind you. On the flipside, don't make your approach, be it via a targeted query letter or as part of a short conversation at a pitch event, listing your sixteen most current and successful screenplays.

Such hefty numbers will do little more than ring the alarm bells for those listening. Even if you've written as many in all your years trying to break through, pepper your creative résumé with your four or five best scripts, and leave the rest at home.

A writer with endless great scripts that have never been produced tells the listening executive that one of two things is likely true:

- The writer does not know a great screenplay from one that is bad or mediocre, and therefore thinks that everything he touches is good.

- The writing may be very good, but there is a personality issue, which is why the writer holds sixteen great scripts that remain unproduced.

If you do have more than a handful of strong screenplays, neither of the above conclusions would be beneficial for you. Pick recent material that shows the most promise, and use it to make your focused push.

## TV Pilot

Once upon a time, TV was the place where film writers went to die. But since Aaron Sorkin, Joss Whedon, and Seth MacFarlane (to name a few), TV has become fertile creative ground. Representation, too, is eager to find writers whose voices and ideas can translate to multiple mediums. In fact, one of the big agencies now works almost exclusively in TV Lit. This is a testament to the fact that, in today's market, TV is where the money is.

If you want to become a TV writer, you will need at least one outstanding TV pilot, accompanied by a complete six-to-twelve-episode bible, which would detail the evolution of your plot and characters from episode to episode over the season's span. As with your film screenplay, make sure your TV pilot is thoroughly vetted and comprehensively thought out, presenting unique characters and interesting new "worlds" to explore that are sure to attract worthwhile television talent.

The TV spec, which used to be much more popular and therefore required, is an alternative to the pilot if you haven't zeroed in on your winning original idea for a TV show yet. In this day and age, TV specs are most often used for applying to a TV writing fellowship. Remember, most TV specs initially come to serve as little more than a sample, proving that you are able to aptly extend and embellish on a preexisting narrative and world. Therefore, you want to keep your specs current, building and expanding upon shows in today's primetime schedule.

## Big Ideas

Powerful cinematic ideas are a Hollywood writer's lifeblood. And big ideas? The truly big ones can translate to money in the bank. My friend Dwayne Smith, a professional screenwriter and published novelist, is known for saying that without a big idea behind it, even the best screenplay will only have so much to offer its audience.

When working with clients, I regularly encourage them to make the cultivation of cinematic ideas part of the regular discipline of their craft. After all, those big ideas will be your saving grace when, at an industry meeting or event an executive will ask, "What else have you got?" Those powerful, thought out, cinematic ideas will be the fuel that powers you.

At any given time, have five (that is, *at least five*) vetted ideas that fall within your brand in your arsenal. A vetted idea is not as simple as a logline. Make sure you write out an outline, or at the very least a Blake Snyder–style beat-sheet, before the idea is ever talked about. Make sure your idea is cinematic in nature and easily lends itself to an escalating story format fitting a three-act structure. You'll need to look no further than your beat-sheet to know whether or not it will survive the test.

## The DIY Project Marketing Kit

For the sake of your own communication about your screenplay, it's important that you have a clear understanding of how your film will be marketed. The better you understand this, the easier it will be to communicate.

Ask yourself: Who would star in this movie or show? What faces do I see on the poster? What genre does it fall in? What are the big trailer moments? And how have other films or TV projects in this genre been marketed, released, or broadcast?

A question I often hear asked of writers is: Who would pay money to see this movie? What is the target demographic for your TV pilot? If you're not sure who your audience is, it's likely that an executive reading your script would be perplexed as well. Sure, everyone dreams of writing a movie or TV show that could be effectively marketed to the four quadrants (male, female, under twenty-five, over twenty-five), but that is rarely the case. Therefore, it's important to know who is likely to pay money to see your movie, or tune in to see your show, and know that sector's moviegoing or television viewing behavior. For example, if you're writing a movie for the over-fifty sector, it will have to be produced on a lower budget, as that sector is known for spending significantly less money than its younger counterparts in the movie theater.

### Track EVERYTHING: Your Excel Document

The entertainment industry tracks everything. And so should you. Even if you don't have the funds for a newfangled online database, or a FileMaker Pro wiz to build you your own, there are plenty of ways to handle your tracking needs effectively.

If you are an iPerson (iPhone, iPad, or Mac), you can turn to a plethora of apps out there to help you track your contacts for your purposes. Just days after I suggested to my client Jocelyne that she organize her contacts that way, she imported all of her institutional knowledge and phone numbers collected on scraps of paper onto a brand-spanking-new contact management app she found for her iPad. The app helped her access information and efficiently cultivate her contacts with all the necessary and superfluous facts, such as when meetings took place and what material was sent, to great effect.

What you want to track is this: your contacts, their information, where and when you met, and any materials, be it completed screenplay, TV pilots, TV specs, or early-stage ideas that you shared with them.

While initially such contacts are few, and creatively driven conversations at best infrequent, over time you will amass a slew of contacts, be they industry executives or other writers, with whom you shared completed works and ideas. If you haven't the funds for an app, keep information about what you shared and with whom in an Excel spreadsheet.

This will save you the embarrassment of sending someone your screenplay twice, or not knowing what someone's talking about when he reaches out to you three months post-meeting pondering the idea you shared with him. Once you've secured representation, your agent and/or manager will keep their own breakdowns of everyone they sent your material to. Until such point, and even long after, it is up to you to stay in the know and on top of the information. It is simply the sign of an informed professional.

# Chapter Twelve

# OH, THE PAPERWORK!

In the entertainment industry, your signature (and occasionally the services of an entertainment lawyer) may be required long before you get to see your name up in lights. Here's a quick breakdown of the paperwork coming your way as you get your work out there.

## Release Forms

While some representation and production companies may accept unsolicited material (i.e., material that did not arrive via representation companies or colleagues), don't be surprised if you are required to sign a release form before your material is accepted.

This is standard practice. By having you sign a release form, the company ensures that it is not opening itself up for backlash by receiving your material. Many companies may already have similar properties in development or production, or represent clients who have similar material. Collecting your release form prior to submission assures them that they are not opening themselves up for litigation should there be a conflict of interest.

Most release forms provide some variation of standard legal language. Still, you should always read material carefully, as you never know when a surprise may be hidden among the verbiage. No need to get your law degree, pay lawyer fees, or take a course in reviewing contracts; simply be diligent about anything you sign.

## Option Agreements

Option agreements allow production entities to test the waters with your material without making a hefty financial investment. An option allows a production entity to "run" with the material exclusively for a set amount of time, and explore whether they are able to attach elements (i.e., name director or actors) or raise capital (i.e., funding) for the project.

Option agreements come in many forms. Some receive an option "memo," while others are delivered an extensive contract. At its core, an option agreement grants the production entity exclusive rights to the material for a defined period of time, and lays the groundwork for financial compensation and rights distribution should the option convert to a sale.

For more on script options, turn to Chapter 25.


## Sale Agreement

Every writer dreams of selling his screenplay; a cash-for-product exchange that will put your career on a whole new track. But selling a script is not like selling a car. There are many elements to be considered there. From merchandising to the rights of the writer to further development of the work, all will be taken into account when your contract is negotiated.

The good news? By the time you get to a sale, you should have an agent, or at the very least a highly competent entertainment lawyer working on your behalf. Even if the production company or studio is eager to introduce you to its lawyers, make sure you have someone versed in entertainment law looking out for your best interest.

While a first script sale will rarely bring in the sort of perks established A-listers get (including rewrite guarantees, set visits, and a small taste of the backend), your first script sale should be negotiated by two informed parties and in good faith.

To learn more about contract minimums, check out the WGA's informative site *www.wga.org*. You will find what you're looking for under Writer's Resources > Contracts & Compensation.

### What's the Backend?

Often, we hear people talk about the backend. So-and-so sold his script for $500,000 with more coming from the backend. The production will make its money back on the backend. James Cameron forfeited his salary and will only receive money from the backend.

The backend refers to something very simple: the movie's returns, i.e., the revenue generated by the cinematic product created from your screenplay. Backend is generally calculated from the net, i.e., after all costs are recovered and mandatory fees are paid.

A handful of A-list actors receive backend money from "first dollar," meaning the backend points are calculated from the gross, as soon as the first movie ticket sells. For writers, it is customary to see a backend point (point = percentage point) or two off the net. These should be negotiated as part of your contract. But you should know that unless the movie was made for a moderate budget and is a big financial success, you should not expect to see a lot of money there.

### Representation: Getting Signed

While everyone wants to "get signed," few representation companies today actually provide their clients with paperwork. Though some (usually agencies) will provide you with paper outlining basic expectations, such as term of representation (twelve months, twenty-four months, etc.), agency fees, payment distribution, and the steps required to break the agreement (for example, a thirty-day written notice prior to the anniversary date), others, most typically management companies, do not paper their deals, leaving you to make sense of the relationship yourself.

When a representation relationship ensues, identify the parameters of your relationship with your new rep. Are they representing a particular project, or representing you as a writer and therefore all of your IP (intellectual properties)? Are you being officially represented, or is this a hip-pocket situation?

For further definitions of potential representation relationships, look to Chapter 19.

Chapter Thirteen

# GETTING YOUR SCREENPLAY OUT THERE

A screenwriting career doesn't happen with the snap of the fingers. As one of my long-term clients is prone to saying, "You have to do the work so you can *do the work*."

So... on to the work!

### Getting Read: Your #1 Job

As a writer trying to break into the industry on the merit of a stellar screenplay, your job is getting your screenplay read. Good material finds its way into the right hands. It is your job then to make sure that you give your material as many opportunities as possible to do that.

Some writers may get precious, and fear exposing their work. Worry not. Stealing material is too expensive; producers and production entities are better off paying you for the rights to your material, and then doing with it whatever they want.

While I do not advocate putting your screenplay online for all to see (there is such a thing as overexposure), there is no harm in getting as many relevant people as you can to read your work. Key word: *relevant*. In this industry, everyone, from the low-level assistant to the high-profile executive, wants to be associated with good material. So do the legwork to stimulate interest. After all, this is the only way to convert fans for your work, the foundation on which your career will be built.

### How Long Is It Going to Take? Rough Timetables

Every writer wants a timeline around which to begin framing expectations.

The need to know what to expect is entirely understandable, though regretfully, the industry does not come with clear timetables. It would be great to expect a sale within six to twelve months of finishing a "Recommend" screenplay, or to book representation within three months of getting your vetted script out there. But that's just not the way it works.

- Getting noticed — You wrote a great screenplay. But since you got it out... nothing. You sent it to production companies, went to pitch events, but it's been nothing but crickets for your screenplay out there. Time to take a step back. The material, for all of your investment, is just not working for you. Good material should garner some level of attention within three to six active months.

- Securing representation — Though many writers see securing representation as their first and most important task, many take years to get there. Agents will not come on board until you have something ready to sell, while managers will look for a piece that's ready for market, or a unique and apt voice they can develop. With a compelling, current, and expertly executed screenplay, you should allow at least four months to secure representation when engaging the correct channels and getting your material read. If you're failing to gain traction in the representation world, it is likely because the material is not strong enough, or the genre/subject matter is difficult to sell or stimulate interest.

- From "like" to script option — In lieu of a sale, everyone wants a script option. However, before an option is installed, the production company may request rewrites to bring the material to its highest marketable potential. Such was exactly the case for a writing team I work with, when their sci-fi thriller gained interest from a prominent NYC production company. Though there is no guarantee that you will receive a script option at its conclusion, it is in your best interest to provide such requested rewrites to build a collaborative relationship and better your chances for a script option for the work. The process of rewrites can take anywhere from a few months to over a year.

- The development process — Ever heard of "development hell"? It's not called that for nothing. Many times, a screenplay that enters the development process, script purchase and all, can end up spending years in development, without ever making it to the screen. A short, active development process, in which notes are given, the screenplay developed, actors and directors come on board and request more script changes, etc., is likely to last as few as one to two years, as many as seven to eight. DreamWorks purchased the rights to the unpublished manuscript behind *Lincoln* in 2001. The film did not go into production until ten years later, in 2011.

- Seeing a movie made of your screenplay — Though many writers hope to finish a screenplay and within a year see it on the screen, even in the best-case scenario it takes years. Chris Terrio's *Argo*, which was based on an article published in 2007 and fast tracked once Ben Affleck was on board, took four years to get from script to screen. The script was first introduced in 2008 — it did not make it to the screen until 2012.

## And Then THIS Happened

A best-case scenario chart for potential, best-case-scenario results from effective, successful actions in the industry.

**Note:** The chart on the following page illustrates BEST-CASE-SCENARIO RESULTS.

# YOU WRITE A SUPERIOR, ORIGINAL, MARKETABLE SCREENPLAY

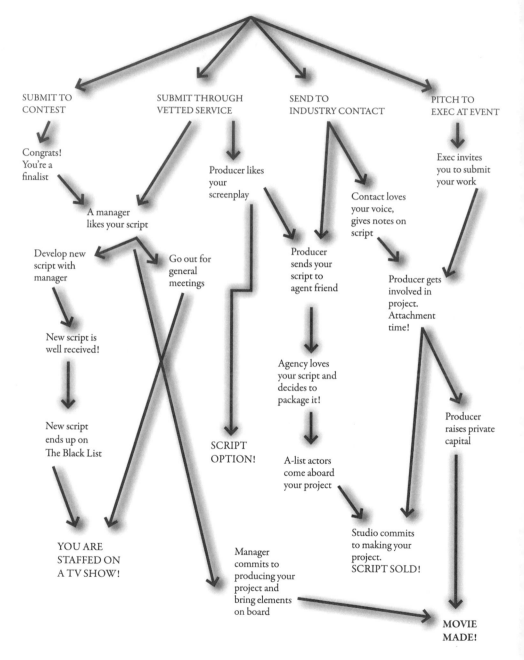

SUBMIT TO CONTEST

SUBMIT THROUGH VETTED SERVICE

SEND TO INDUSTRY CONTACT

PITCH TO EXEC AT EVENT

Congrats! You're a finalist

Producer likes your screenplay

Contact loves your voice, gives notes on script

Exec invites you to submit your work

A manager likes your script

Develop new script with manager

Go out for general meetings

Producer sends your script to agent friend

Producer gets involved in project. Attachment time!

New script is well received!

Agency loves your script and decides to package it!

Producer raises private capital

New script ends up on The Black List

SCRIPT OPTION!

A-list actors come aboard your project

YOU ARE STAFFED ON A TV SHOW!

Manager commits to producing your project and bring elements on board

Studio commits to making your project. SCRIPT SOLD!

MOVIE MADE!

## Building Your Network

A few years ago, I was invited by Final Draft to moderate a screenwriting panel for the Hollywood Black Film Festival. Antwone Fisher (yes, THAT Antwone Fisher) was on the panel, and when asked by the audience if at this stage of his career he could just sit back and let the work come to him, he told the audience that while he had an agent, a manager, a lawyer, and a publicist, they did not get him his jobs. I found this amazing. Antwone had this whole team, and yet they didn't get him writing jobs?

After the panel, Antwone and I got to talking. I had to figure out how it was that he secured himself all of his own work, despite having a powerful writer's dream team at his disposal. That was when Antwone explained to me that, with all the networking he's done consistently and effectively, the jobs came straight to him. Antwone, it turned out, was consistently collecting business cards at events and meetings, and sending a follow up thank-you card to everyone he came across. When it came time for powerful players to hire the right person for the job, they remembered Antwone favorably, and came straight to him. Of course, this did not happen every time. But the relationships that Antwone forged were strong enough so that his agent did not need to facilitate them.

What Antwone pointed out is simple: a little courtesy goes a long way in this industry. Take the name of every person you meet, and put those names in your database, even if it's just a glorified spreadsheet concocted in Excel. And by meet, I mean come across. Attend their lectures. Participate in their webinars. Have five minutes with them at pitching events. The entertainment industry is made entirely of strangers; don't be afraid to reach out in a professional, respectful way. As my friend, aspiring writer/director and expert networker TJ Mino, once pointed out, most people in this industry remember what it was like before they made it, and are happy to help out.

But building your network is not about getting people within the industry to do things for you; it's about building your community within this very social environment. Reach out to those who are one or five steps ahead of where you are — working writers or ones who have gotten some attention like a contest win or a placement on The Black List. Tell them why you're reaching out — you liked their last project, responded to something specific they said in a webinar or lecture, or are a fan of their body of work. Offer to buy them a cup of coffee. Get to know them and learn from their journeys. If they feel you are genuine, in time they will extend a helping hand without your having to ask for one.

### Local Opportunities on the East and West Coast

If you live on the East or West Coast, specifically Los Angeles or New York, opportunities are ample to meet industry folks. Be it pitch events, industry panels, or screenwriting conferences, there is plenty going on. Keep your eye out for local events that are of interest, and use those to connect with other writers and potential industry contacts.

Los Angeles offers major screenwriting events most months of the year. These events are perfect opportunities to meet industry executives and junior-level creative and representation types. Guilds such as the WGA, DGA, and PGA, as well as ATAS (Academy of Television Arts and Science) often put on events as well as offer opportunities for writers to listen to panels and observe lectures on both coasts. These are perfect places to meet industry executives and other aspirants like you. For Los Angeles locals, here are a few event-driven resources:

- Writers Guild Foundation (*www.wgfoundation.org*) — Part of the WGA, the foundation organizes a lot of writer-driven events with great speakers.

- Academy of Television Arts & Sciences (*www.emmys.tv*) —The organization puts on some great writer-driven TV-related events.

- The Writing Pad (*www.writingpad.com*) — This Los Angeles–based organization puts on panels, writers' drink nights, and lots of other writer-centric events.

New York, too, now offers a number of relevant conferences throughout the year, as well as WGA East events. Check out your calendar and review event materials to identify the events that are right for you.

You will find relevant, industry-related events in other cities as well. Chicago, Seattle, San Francisco, and Boston, to name a few, have local organizations that work hard to bring in industry executives, and film festivals, big and small, are popping up everywhere.

Film schools, be they independent or university driven, often put on lectures and screenings complete with panels and guest teachers. So do major publications in support of a new movie coming out or a project filming locally. Look to film festivals to connect with other writers and industry types, coming out in support of a project or to network with one another.

### Building Your Network Via Email and Phone

Email is every writer's friend. It is unobtrusive, and doesn't demand the same personal heft as phone communication. And, when you're sending an email, no one knows whether you're doing so from one area code over, or halfway across the country.

Don't be shy about crafting a thoughtful, respectful email to ones you've met, thanking them for their time. The worst-case scenario is that they will hit delete without ever sending an answer your way. In that case, you can always reach out once you have a new screenplay ready to share or when you place in a contest a few months later, and invite your contact to read your work. As long as you remain consistent, professional, and relevant, you are likely to attract their attention sooner or later.

Communicating with your network via email or phone consistently (but not doggedly) allows you to stay front-of-mind whether you are local or remote. Remember not to start every conversation talking about the difference in weather or the hour it is in your time zone, and they will forgive the fact that you would not be available to drive over at a moment's notice. But know that when the time comes and THAT opportunity arises, you should be ready and willing to travel, and cover the cost.

Chapter Fourteen

# QUERY LETTERS

If you've been trying to break into the industry for a while, chances are you've written a query letter. Or you've been told to write a query letter by someone along the way. The problem? Most query letters are no longer being read.

## A Brief History

Back in the long gone '80s and early '90s, query letters were THE way to get out there. All you had to do was reach for your latest copy of the *Hollywood Creative Directory* (which has since folded), pull out the names of representation firms and production companies to approach, print out some mailing labels and BAM! Query letters everywhere.

This was, for many, the fastest way to get discovered. You send a query letter in, an agent or a producer likes one of your loglines and asks to see your screenplay. The script is great? A connection is made. For a while, every major agency and production company had someone dedicated to covering the "query desk." The problem? With the Internet once again making our universe flat, screenwriters, seasoned and wholly inexperienced, started popping up everywhere. And with them came a flood of query letters that became nearly impossible to keep up with.

For a while, it was the interns' or assistants' job to keep up with query letters. But by the time someone got to your query letter, identified the script they wanted to read, and came around to requesting... time had passed. Soon, that person would go back to school, move on to his next job or a better desk, and the query pile got assigned to somebody else.

### Query Letter Sending Services

I am not going to make many friends here but... what the hell. I'm more than happy to keep loyal to services whose business models I think work. Query letter distribution services? Well, if query letters are no longer being widely read, despite all the services that swear that they will deliver your query letter to hundreds of companies... you do the math. Just because it gives you something to do, doesn't mean it's going to get you anywhere.

'Nuff said.

### Why General Queries Don't Work

At the height of the query letter craze, agents, managers, and producers were receiving upward of five hundred queries a week. Between servicing existing clients and reading screenplays recommended by business associates, most production and representation companies eventually gave up any methodical dedication to sifting through queries, and found more certain, vetted paths to finding quality screenplays.

Part of the problem is this: most anyone could proclaim to be a screenwriter. Most anyone could learn how to put together an adequate query letter. But delivering a strong screenplay? That's a whole other bowl of wax. The work that the query letter promotes became too much of an unknown. Because, with the help of software, most anyone can make a few bound sheets of paper look like a screenplay, sifting through all the bad material in the hopes of uncovering a good script simply became too much work.

While agents and producers rarely read cold query letters these days, I do on occasion talk to managers still dedicated to finding that great, undiscovered screenplay this way, and who therefore on occasion still read query letters. Even then, the ratio of query letters to read request is roughly 500 to 1. Those are not particularly good odds to play.

### Targeted Query Letters

One type of query letter that could potentially work: the hyper-targeted query letter. We are talking about a query letter that has been completely tailored to the reader on the other end. While there are no guarantees that such a query letter will receive a response or even get read, here are a few pointers for writing such a query, which could potentially stimulate interest for your work:

- Research the person you're querying. — You have something in common? Went to the same school or grew up in the same small town? Put it in there.

- Why is this person receiving your query? — Has this person produced a movie you loved? Does this person represent a writer of whom you're a big fan? Be clear about why you've chosen to approach this person.

- It's about the work. — Unless it's completely relevant (like a person whose last name is Green sending a query letter on green paper), leave the shticks out of it.

- Don't hide your successes. — You've won a contest, sold a screenplay, or been optioned? Make sure the reader knows why he should be paying attention.

While there are no guarantees, use these guidelines for targeted queries, and you just might be able to garner interest from a select few for your work.

# Chapter Fifteen

# SCREENWRITING CONTESTS

Placing as a finalist in an established, industry-driven contest can undoubtedly open doors for your work. Evan Daugherty, who wrote *Snow White and the Huntsman*, was discovered by my friend, manager Jake Wagner, when Evan won the Script Pipeline contest, while Larry Brenner's *Bethlehem*, a finalist in 2010's Big Break contest, was recently sold to Universal with Joe Roth attached to produce.

Only a handful of contests deliver these stellar results, while others leave placers enjoying a triumph that doesn't often lead to much more. In this chapter, we will explore the contests that you should be entering, and how to position every success for maximum results.

## Screenwriting Contests 101

Screenwriting contests have been around for some time. The Nicholl Fellowship, the industry's single most respectable contest-type brand, which awarded its prestigious fellowship to writers of such gems as *Akeelah and the Bee* and *Finding Forrester*, was launched in 1985, and continues to accept entries every year to this day.

Through the years, many contests have come and gone. While the right contest can certainly help writers gain the attention they deserve, it has proven challenging for mid-size contests to stay relevant. In recent years, bigger contests have continued to solidify their reputation, while smaller contests have often faded away if they failed to make a real splash. A number of new contests have popped up, but only a few, like Tracking B's annual contest, have managed to really set themselves apart from the pack.

Today, it is up to the writer to determine not only which contests you might be able to win, but also to understand which wins would translate to industry success.

**Everything You Need to Know, and Everywhere You Go to Find It**

In order to know which contest to enter, you have to know where to do your research. Here is a list of resources to help you set your annual screenplay-submission budget and schedule:

- *MovieBytes.com* —This site may not have the most cutting-edge look, but it still delivers consistent information about contest deadlines and fees, as well as a comprehensive directory and contest-related news.

- *WithoutABox.com* — Serving as a popular submission portal for many screenwriting contests, this site, owned by Amazon, offers detailed information for the contests it promotes.

- *ScreenplayContests.com* — With a name so obvious, how could you go wrong? This site offers a comprehensive directory, as well as some interesting contest-related articles and blogs.

**The Best-Established Screenplay Contests**

If you've taken even a moment to glance at the sites I mentioned in the previous section, then surely you've noticed: there are so many contests out there! How do you know which to choose? While I can't list every contest that has delivered something of worth, the contests featured below have produced, year after year, stellar results:

- The Nicholl Fellowship — Launched by the Academy of Motion Picture Arts and Sciences to help identify emerging writers of worth, this contest receives upward of 6,000 entries each year and is considered the cream of the crop. In addition to having a number of winning screenplays produced, Nicholl Fellows have gone on to be awarded Pultizer Prizes, and receive nominations for Academy Awards.

- Final Draft's Big Break Contest — Final Draft's annual contest receives 6,500+ submissions in both television and film categories. The finalists receive prizes and visibility, with the winners getting flown to Los Angeles, celebrated in Final Draft's annual gala, and escorted to meetings with A-list executives. Winners have sold screenplays, secured representation, and become working professionals.

- Austin Film Festival Screenplay & Teleplay Competition — With over 6,000 combined entries, this competition has quickly gained a strong reputation for not only giving the winners a great platform, but also producing top-notch winners.

- TrackingB Script Contest — A relative newbie (first winners were announced in 2007), this contest focuses entirely on industry access. Accepting both film and TV submissions, the contest sets out to gain representation for as many of its finalists as possible, promoting the top three scripts on TrackingB's industry-staple script tracking board. The New Wave prize matches one lucky writer with management.

Other big contests that deliver great value include:

- The Page International Screenwriting Contest — Lots of writers got repped, optioned, and produced as a result of this contest.

- Script Pipeline — A trusted industry contest known for its "insider" reputation; managers look to the winners and finalists of this contest for worthwhile new talent.

- Blue Cat Screenwriting Contest — Created by writers, and boasting a reputation for discovering fantastic talent!

Television fellowships, for those trying to break into television via these prestigious positions, are offered by the following:

- CBS Writers Mentoring Program
- Disney/ABC Television Writing Program

- Fox Writers Intensive
- NBC/Universal's Writers on the Verge
- Nickelodeon Writing Program
- WB's Writers' Workshop

**Other Noteworthy Screenwriting Contests**

While big wins in big contests often yield big rewards, here are some of the mid-size and smaller contests that are worth looking into:

- American Zoetrope — Who doesn't want to get read by Francis Ford Coppola?

- CineStory — Connects CineStory Fellows with working Hollywood mentors in an exclusive CineStory retreat.

- Screamfest Screenplay Competition — If you write horror, this might just be the competition for you!

- Slamdance Screenwriting and Teleplay Competition — Once Sundance became virtually unwinnable for unknown writers, Slamdance became a great avenue for new scribes.

There are plenty more out there! Do the research and identify the screenwriting competition that's right for you.

**Considering a Screenwriting Contest? What to Look For**

Nobody is going to get rich winning screenwriting contests. When it comes to the bigger contests the money is nice, but not ultimately why you enter. So when you are considering a screenwriting contest, what should you be looking for?

- Reputation — If the screenwriting contest does not have big past wins (getting writers repped by a name agency or management company or getting the winning material optioned by a reputable production company), the industry will not be looking to see who they've discovered this year.

- Who's reading the finalists? — The reason to enter any screenwriting contest is to get your script read by reputable industry executives. Make a point to know who's reading the scripts that make it to the finals.

- Relevance — Is this a contest that is relevant to the entertainment industry? If it's all prizes but no real industry connections are mentioned, it likely wouldn't garner you the recognition you want.

- Big Fish/Big Pond — Winning or placing in a contest is all about establishing yourself as the big fish in the big pond. Entering contests where you might have better odds of winning will not help you if the contest itself has no clout. Marketing yourself as the winner of the Schenectady Screenwriting Contest (if there is one) might not actually work in your favor; it indicates you might not know the contests that are looked to, and could end up working against you.

- Know the numbers — Are you entering a competition with 300 or 3,000 entries? The number of scripts you beat to get to the top can make all the difference.

### Festival-Based Contests

More and more relevant film festivals have rolled out screenwriting contests in recent years. From Nantucket to New Hampshire and Big Bear, film festivals have made screenwriting contests a meaningful component of their program.

Film festivals offer a fantastic opportunity to highlight industry projects and executives, while creating occasions for aspirants to connect with those who are steps and leaps ahead. Much as with straight contests, when considering entering your screenplay into a contest associated with a festival, research who will be reading your work. The right festivals offer ample opportunities to connect with industry executives in an incubated and focused environment.

## Work It: Becoming a Finalist

Entering a screenwriting contest is not, necessarily, about winning. Let me say it again, in a slightly different way: in order to capitalize on your placement in a contest you don't have to win — you have to be a finalist. Congratulations! As there are usually five to ten scripts on the finalists' list, your chances for success just increased significantly.

Back in my ScriptShark days, I ran a contest myself, and had the finalists judged by industry executives. One particular year, two executives expressed interest in the material they read before we announced the winners. One of the finalists secured representation before the top five placers were announced. Another began developing his screenplay with an Academy Award–nominated producer who read his work as part of the finalists' stack. Ironically, neither of these writers won the top prize. But the all-important industry inroads were already paved.

While everyone loves a winner, most everyone in the industry looks at a big contest's finalists' list. Reaching the top five or the top ten is plenty to convince those in the industry that your screenplay might just be worth a look.

## Winning the Top Prize

Being a finalist is great. Being named the winner? Fantastic!

Your script is the one that beat everyone else's, and while finalists will receive recognition and interest, being named the winner brings with it a whole other level of accolades. Marketing yourself as the winner of, say, Final Draft's Big Break Contest, is a powerful conversation starter. For at least a year, market yourself as "Winner of," ensuring that this information is displayed front and center in any outreach efforts, pitches, and targeted queries. If you win any of the contests listed in this book, you will gain instant interest from many executives.

## Contest Wins Expire: Capitalizing on Your Momentum

In one of my contest-running years at ScriptShark, I crowned a

*The winners of Final Draft's 2012's Big Break contest*

contest winner unanimously voted into the top spot by my panel of industry judges. Agents, managers, and executives wanted to meet this guy. Since he was out-of-state, we started making arrangements for his promised trip to Los Angeles and consequent industry meetings, all part of his prize package. My winner stalled. Postponed his trip by a few weeks. Then by a couple of months. After which he stopped responding to my emails.

Two years later, just as I was getting ready to announce that year's winner, I got the call: "I'm ready to come out now." Calmly, I explained to my twice-removed winner that, in accordance with the rules, I was no longer obligated to provide him with an industry trip, as he did not take advantage of his prize in the time allotted. "I'll come anyway. Let's set some meetings up," he said.

What this contest winner had to have explained, eventually with pretty harsh words, is this: if you won a contest but didn't do anything with your win for two years, that win is gone. There are now new winners with new promise whom everyone is excited about. Unless you were in a coma, not having done anything with your win for two years is effectively industry suicide. You're better off starting from scratch than telling executives that you were handed a way in but ultimately didn't feel like doing anything with it until now.

## The Art of the Spin

Placement is placement. It's up to you what you do with it. You didn't win the top prize but made finalist? No matter. Everything can, and often should be, spun.

Within the realm of reason, executives will look to you to see how you regard the accomplishments you've amassed. You didn't win Page but made it into the Top 20? That's Top 20 from 6,000+ screenplays. It's up to you whether to hang your head in shame or make the best of it knowing that Top 20 in Page is held in high regard despite the fact that it's not where you wanted to end up.

## Making the Most of Every Win

The biggest mistake writers make once they win or place in a high-value contest? Wait for the contest provider to do everything on their behalf.

When I escorted last year's Big Break contest winners to their industry meetings, the grand prize winner said to me, "As far as I'm concerned, what they do for me ends in these three days of industry meetings. From here on out, it's in my hands." Even though Final Draft's Shelly Mellott continued to work for her winners long after their meetings were over, this particular contest winner took a very beneficial stance.

Don't wait for organizers to make things happen. They will do what they can, but eventually have to move on to administrating their next annual contest. Take the win and run with it. Contact everyone you can. Let them know that you have won or placed in a high-profile contest, and invite them to read your work. Then, when your follow-up script is ready to share, contact them again, and remind them of the contest wins under your belt.

Bottom line? No one will benefit more than you from the exposure winning or placing in a high-profile screenwriting contest can generate. If you got the win, it's up to you to put it to work.

Chapter Sixteen

# LISTING AND
# RECOMMENDATION SERVICES

Logic says that getting your screenplay read should be so much easier in the age of the Internet, where information is fluid, and everything made so easily accessible. The challenge: overflow of incoming material has bogged down many an executive. Hence, it's important to know where to go to get noticed, to ensure that any financial investment is well spent.

## Listing Services

Listing services seem like a natural fit with the global adoption of the Internet. While they may not have become the beacons of new material many originally saw as their inevitable fate, they do serve an important and valuable purpose.

### *What Are Listing Services?*

Listing services are online repositories or databases of available screenplays, accessible to industry executives to sift through for worthwhile writers and materials. First introduced in the late '90s, listing services allow writers to post profiles of their projects consisting of anything from loglines to synopses and coverage, based on the service's unique parameters, with the aim of stimulating interest in the material from industry executives. Listing is provided for a monthly or annual fee. Most such services allow writers to make their screenplays available for download.

Today's most popular listing services include:

- The Black List — Launched by Franklin Leonard of The Black List fame, this listing service allows writers to post profiles of their work, and offers proprietary coverage and scoring models to help quality material make its way up the ranks. In operation since October 2012, the listing service gained immediate interest from industry executives due to the strong built-in brand. I consistently hear from representation counterparts they've gone back to the site looking for quality writers again and again, trusting the site for quality screenplays.

- Spec Scout — Jason Scoggins' listing service is different in that it doesn't invite every writer to list his material; rather, it invites writers to submit their material for a collection of three coverages for a nominal fee. If the coverages return high marks, the writer is then invited to list his material alongside represented material and material written by known writers making headway in the industry.

- InkTip — The oldest listing service out there (launched in the early 2000s), InkTip has a solid and specific reputation. While it no longer holds the shine of some of the newer services, it does offer consistent success stories specific to producers and production companies finding material on the site, as well the occasional management company or agency win.

### Managing Expectations

Many writers expect that as soon as their screenplay hits a listing service, the emails will come flooding in. Executives generally know what they are looking for; they have either a genre or a writer type in mind. Of course, the better your script scores, the more likely you are to garner all-important interest. But even then, material that falls within a popular genre is more likely to get read.

While executives certainly keep an eye out for new material listed with a given service, keeping track of newly listed scripts and new writers is not the primary part of the job for any of them; that said, they are always on the lookout, and a trusted source can become a consistent destination for many. Specifically in a situation like The Black List or Spec Scout where material's already been vetted, executives appreciate being able to look through material that, with the help of scoring systems, has already been filtered for them. On The Black List's listing service, elements such as material rating (provided only to those screenplays submitted for coverage) compute into the attention a piece of material receives, while popular genres always tend to be more heavily in demand. In addition, both The Black List and Spec Scout publish a weekly newsletter highlighting highly-ranked material, giving qualifying writers one more avenue for much needed attention.

### The Danger of Listing Services

While seemingly harmless, there are a number of dangers listing services pose to the writer listing material. Those dangers do not include material theft. While an idea (IP or intellectual property) is impossible to register, a screenplay should be protected via the usual avenues mentioned earlier.

The real dangers of listing services are these:

- The illusion of activity — Listing services often give the writer the illusion of active engagement. While your screenplay may one day be discovered through a listing service, the odds are not ultimately in your favor. If you choose to list your material with such a service, do so and quickly turn your attention to other endeavors in which you can more consistently and proactively participate.

- Overexposure — Material can be overexposed and, by extension, grow stale. Be mindful of when you first list your screenplay, and what sort of attention it's received since being listed.

If it has not received notable attention since being listed and a few months have passed, consider taking it down if only so it doesn't go stale.

### *Deciphering Which Listing Service Is Right for You*

You want to know which listing service is worth your hard-earned cash? Take a look at their success stories. It's as simple as that. Whether they are listed right on the site or can be found on a DoneDealPro message-board string, the information is out there for the uncovering. Look for names you recognize, or companies that turn up in simple research without a lot of detective work. The point of listing your material with such a service is to connect with those who are further along than you are in their endeavors.

## Recommendation Services

Recommendation services are those that actively recommend or "scout" your material to industry executives and companies. Many such services exist as an extension of a coverage service. Both ScriptShark and ScriptXpert, to name a few, recommend screenplays that receive the coveted "Consider" or "Recommend" rating to their industry contacts.

### *Managing Expectations*

Having your material recommended to industry executives through an established, reputable service can gain you exposure and facilitate introductions. During my time at ScriptShark, I secured representation, landed options, and created relationships for writers just this way. A scouting service is ordinarily known for its effective readers, able to identify quality material that is market ready, and therefore delivering material to executives that is already vetted.

On occasion, services will get backed up and take time to scout your script. Don't fret! They are managing their industry relationships for your benefit. If they sent out loglines twice a day, eventually the executives would get in the habit of hitting "delete"; they have tons of vetted material coming at them as is. So trust that the service knows what it's doing, and turn your attention to marketing efforts in which you can more actively participate.

Know this: scouting is, in most cases, a onetime deal. The service will get the logline of your material out, along with some project/writer highlights to its executives, send the script in to those who go on to request it, then move on to the next screenplay on the list. If your material was scouted but did not receive interest, it is time to move on to your next effort.

### How Do Recommendation Services Work?

A recommendation service uses its coverage channels by identifying "Consider" and "Recommend" screenplays for its scouting services. Therefore, script ratings are nonnegotiable and under great scrutiny; it's of the utmost importance to a recommendation service that the screenplays it introduces to the industry are ones that can garner real interest. If quality is compromised, executives will soon stop reading material from the service and therefore dilute the service's ability to act on behalf of its "Recommend" and "Consider" writers.

### Are Recommendation Services Worth Your Money?

No matter what, never pay for recommendations. The services that do it in a worthwhile fashion do it based on their reputation for high-quality material; high quality and compensation simply do not mix. Services like those mentioned above will get you interest based on their track record and integrity. If they're asking for your money outside of the pay for coverage, chances are something's amiss.

### The Dangers of Recommendation Services

Like listing services, recommendation services give the writer the illusion of doing something actively. Writers wait with bated breath, eager to see what happens when their screenplay is finally scouted to the industry. While you should certainly keep tabs on where your script might be on the scouting queue and when it's due to go out to the company's industry list, it should be one of many efforts you're pursuing.

Chapter Seventeen

# THE ART OF THE PITCH

A scribe put off by the industry's expectation that a writer should know how to efficiently pitch once wrote to me, "Pitching is for baseball," followed by a five-letter expletive. And while he and the industry clearly differ on where the term best fits, there is one thing worth noting here: as in baseball, where no one hits a homerun on a whim, pitching a screenplay, no matter how brief, is a craft, one that should be practiced and honed repeatedly in order to make sure that when up to bat, the writer will deliver effectively.

In the writer's toolbox, little will garner as much attention as the all-important pitch. While in some scenarios a pitch speaks to your thought-out narrative summation of your cinematic masterpiece, in others pitching is just a fancy way of framing the manner in which you talk about your script. Entire books have been dedicated to this subject. Weekend seminars taught. Consultants engaged. Despite my best intentions, there is just no way to boil it all down to a single chapter. Therefore, this chapter will serve as a broad foundation.

## Not All Screenplays Are Created Equal: What Type of Script Is Pitchable?

Some screenplays were born for a pitch. They have the magical ability to materialize for the listener and trigger his imagination in a couple of sentences or less. Others? Not so much. The more story-heavy, execution-dependent your script, the harder it is going to be to pitch. The simpler, more accessible it is, the easier it will be to deliver straight down the middle.

As a rule of thumb, high-concept or contained material is the easiest to pitch. It rests on the shoulders of a strong idea, which should be instantly accessible for the listener. What if aliens attacked Earth on the 4th of July? What if a serial killer was killing his victims in accordance with the seven deadly sins? What if Romeo and Juliet fell in love aboard the doomed *Titanic*? In no way do these propositions lay out the entire movie, but as soon as you hear it, you get the gist of what the screenplay will be.

This doesn't mean that a non-high concept can't be framed in a stellar pitch. Always think about the major drivers of your material, ones that will be easily accessible for your listener, so that they may identify whether the screenplay holds interest.

## Pitch Types

Different circumstances call for different pitches. It's important to be familiar with the various pitch types, and know when which is appropriate. While you may pitch yourself one way or construct a unique pitch for a television project, below are some of today's most common pitching formats:

- The Elevator Pitch — This is, by far, the pitch type most repeated. Its name is born of the amount of time it should take you to deliver this succinct summary: the length of time it would take for an elevator ride. This pitch style is conversational, focusing on thematic and narrative highlights. Choose your words carefully as you perfect this one — the art here is delivering only the most pertinent information while exciting the listener enough to develop interest in your material.

- The Twenty-Minute Pitch — A more elaborate, act-by-act, major-story-beat by major-story-beat retelling of your story, with crafty weaving of themes to allow the listener to really get a handle on the movie or TV show that your script is laying out before them.

- The Forty-Five-Plus Minute Pitch — The folks who are requested to deliver these are ones who can get into very powerful rooms and have long been working. When the time does come to present such a pitch, be sure to turn to a pitch consultant to help you craft it.

## Pitch Styles

Everyone you talk to has their favored pitch styles, as well as styles they can't bear. For every successful writer who swears that mash-ups — a la *Mean Girls* meets *American Beauty* — work wonders, a pitch coach will likely tell you to never, ever go there. Some will tell you to make it personal. Relatable. Others will advise you to tell it straight. Me? I have my own broad guidelines to share.

- Keep it about the work. — Don't bring in costumes. Don't deliver your pitch as a whimsical limerick. Stick to the script. If you don't, the listener may just assume the work can't speak for itself.

- Bring the funny. — If you're pitching a comedy, make it funny. If it's a thriller you have, make sure you create suspense. Listeners are more likely to ask for the script if they feel you deliver right off the bat.

- The end is in your hands. — Never, ever, ask an executive whether he wants you to tell him the end. If you want to reveal the story's resolution, do it. If you don't, leave it out, but be ready to answer should the listening executive ask.

## Constructing a Powerful Elevator Pitch

Constructing a powerful and compelling one-to-two-minute pitch is no easy task. After all, how do you narrow down ninety-plus pages of content to a ninety-second retelling without compromising the heart of the story, or sounding entirely rushed? This is where you will have to take a step back and ask yourself: what is your screenplay about? Be it story- or theme-driven, that is what you will be tasked with presenting up-front-and-center when you are pitching.

A powerful elevator pitch doesn't focus on the B-plots, or waste time on marginal characters. Instead, it explores what the movie is really about, delivering its essence in a deliberate, thoughtful fashion.

When practicing your pitch, make sure the listener is able to deduce: Who is your protagonist? What is your protagonist's goal? What is your protagonist up against, and what's at stake? And if it's not happening here and now, what world is it set in?

Your conflict should be front and center. Don't spend your time setting up your world and protagonist only to bury the core conflict in your very last sentence. The listener will want to know whether the conflict is one that speaks to him; don't make him work for it.

In a short pitch, a handful of deliberate adjectives can be your best friend. With them, your protagonist can easily go from a "guy in his thirties" to a "disheveled thirty-year-old ingrate," or illustrate your teenage protagonist as one who is "always the good girl." Powerful, revealing information delivered in just a few words.

Clarity is key. Even if the listener doesn't connect with the material, he will be able to appreciate the precision with which you delivered your pitch.

**What Executives Are Listening For**

When listening to a pitch, executives are looking to extract specific information. While they are not looking for you to spell out the following for them or go down a list, they are aiming to infer the answers from your pitch.

- Genre — What genre is your screenplay in? For production companies and development executives, this will help identify whether this is something they would get involved in.

- Casting — What name actors could potentially be cast as your lead, love interest, or antagonist? Be sure to identify the age, gender, and one or two general characteristics (once again, adjectives).

- Budget — Does your script have a lot of explosions? Special effects? Is it a period piece? Make sure this is clear.

- Audience Demographic — Who will be the audience for this movie? Are we talking fan-boys, young women, or retirees? Each demographic has unique moviegoing and TV-viewing behaviors.

Understanding the audience for which the material is intended will help the listener know how it would best be marketed.

- Differentiators — How is your idea the same as successful ones that came before, but different enough to offer something new, unique, and interesting?

## Pitching the Big Idea

The bigger the idea, the simpler the pitch. When you pitch the big idea, the executive listening should be able to see the movie poster, imagine the trailer, and envision the marketing campaign. A big idea is one that is accessible, that makes the listener wonder: how come they haven't done this already? The more details you will tack on it, the more likely you are to complicate it and therefore deter the person listening from expressing interest. As my friend Sheila Hanahan Taylor, partner at Practical Pictures, once told me, executives usually know whether your pitch is of interest to them in the first thirty seconds. If your pitch spans sixty seconds, they will spend the first thirty finding what excites them about the material, and the latter thirty seconds listening for anything that would deter them from reading.

## Pitching Plot vs. Theme

A story about a family's matriarch dying of cancer just doesn't make for an exciting pitch. If you are dealing with an execution-dependent script that is light on plot but heavy on the protagonist's internal journey, you are probably going to be best served sacrificing a little plot for a lot of theme.

In this scenario, you want to talk about what the movie is ABOUT — theme, emotion, larger subject matter — rather then just what the movie — plotlines and all — is about. Instead of telling the listener about a movie in which Joey's mother is diagnosed with terminal cancer, how Joey, unable to deal with his grief, becomes a drunk, then joins a support group just in time for his mother to see him back on the up-and-up before she dies, tell the listener about the powerful story you've constructed examining love, loss, facing our demons, and coming to terms with our own mortality. While this sort of material is never easy to pitch, you will have a much better chance of gaining interest based on the listener connecting emotionally with the themes.

## Pitch Consultants and Teachers

Like screenwriting, pitching requires a methodology with which screenwriters can connect, one that makes sense to them, and in which they can repeatedly succeed. A number of established pitch coaches out there can help you arrive at your perfect pitch.

- Pilar Alessandra — To many, Pilar is as good as it gets. Armed with a tested methodology, Pilar puts her years of industry experience to good use, helping each writer find his way to an effective, powerful pitch.

- Michael Hauge — Story and screenwriting consultant Michael Hauge wrote the renowned book, *Selling Your Story in 60 Seconds*, and is often relied on by large pitching events to deliver his superior pitching class to their pitching enthusiasts.

- Stephanie Palmer/Good in a Room — Stephanie, once a VP of Creative Affairs at MGM, has helped many an A-lister arrive at a perfect pitch. She is insightful, experienced, and a wonderful teacher as well as the author of one of the definitive pitching books, *Good in a Room*.

⁓

Hardly anyone can deliver a killer pitch on a whim, and those who can will certainly not be able to repeat it. Identify the pitching style that works for you, find the pitch coach who suits you, and begin working on crafting this valuable tool.

Chapter Eighteen

# PITCH EVENTS AND PITCH SERVICES

It doesn't take too much scratching of the surface to uncover a pitch event these days. Specifically in Los Angeles but also in New York, pitch events (usually connected with a larger conference) seem to be everywhere. The Great American PitchFest, *Fade In* magazine's Hollywood Pitch Festival, and Screenwriters World (to name a few) have all made a name for themselves, attracting writers from across the nation and around the world eager to present industry executives with their work.

## The Nature of Pitch Events

Pitch events, by nature, are chaotic. Hundreds of writers come to pitch their winning ideas to industry executives, who listen to up to a dozen pitches in an hour, often taking sixty-plus pitches in a single day.

While pitch events may open doors and forge industry connections, they are NOT the place where deals are made. Most of the material pitched at such events will be heavily execution-dependent; rarely will executives hear the type of pitch that will make them stand up and say, "I want to buy that!" There are only a handful of decision makers and greenlighters in the industry in the first place, and for all their good intentions, a pitch event is just not where they're at.

Still, there are plenty of connections of worth to be made at pitch events. After all, where else can you find a roomful of ready and willing agents, managers, development executives, and producers?

The key to your success? Knowing whom you are pitching to, and, just as important, coming prepared.

*Writers pitching at The Great American PitchFest*

### Are Pitch Events Right for You?

Whether you are local or remote, participating in a pitch event requires a significant expense. Even if you're not investing in travel and accommodations, you will be investing in the pitch sessions themselves, and, unless you are set on only doing one or two pitches, those can rack up, fast.

When considering whether to make the time and financial investment in a pitch event, come up with an honest answer to this question: is a pitch event the sort of environment in which you and your material are likely to excel?

To help you find the answer, here are additional questions to ask yourself:

- Are you personable? — If you can't deliver a solid, confident pitch, a pitch event may not be the right way for you to get out there. No one is asking you to become a social butterfly, but those who tend to excel at such events are comfortable in their own skin and build new relationships easily.

- Is your screenplay pitchable? — If your screenplay is one that is lighter on concept and plot, and heavier on personal reflection and theme, it is not likely one that will make waves in a pitch event. Attend a pitch event if you have the sort of pitch that can be memorable without requiring too much setup or narrative explanation.

- Is your screenplay ready to show? — If your screenplay is not ready (and by ready I mean vetted), don't bother with a pitch event. The worst thing you can do is attend a pitch event hoping to get a temperature gauge on a concept you're toying with. As soon as the executive will realize you don't have the actual screenplay, he will lose interest.

Remember, despite your best hopes, pitch events are not right for everyone. Consider the above points honestly when debating whether to make the financial and time investment required for attendance.

## Managing Expectations

You have that highly pitchable, exciting screenplay. You carry yourself well — there is no threat of sudden combustion. At least not while in the room, anyway. You decided to make the investment. So now that you've handed over your credit card, what should you expect?

As mentioned earlier, pitch events are chaotic by nature. Even in the best-run events, when you have upward of fifty executives taking pitches from an equal number of writers in five-minute increments, things are likely to get a little out of hand. Writers will walk in but not be able to locate their executives. Writers from the previous sessions will linger at an executive's desk. Other writers who missed a previous appointment will beg and plead to be fit in for an additional session the executive doesn't have.

Here are a few tips to help make the best of your pitch event:

- Show up on time. — Most problems in pitch events start when people systematically run late. Show up on time, scope out where you have to be and when.

- Know your schedule. — Being unsure of whom you're supposed to pitch to and when creates chaos for those running the room and doesn't bode well with the executives.

- Do your research. — Know whom you're pitching to, and whether your project may hold interest for them.

**The Three (Realistic) Reasons to Attend a Pitch Event**

It's completely human to walk into a pitch event and hope for the best, i.e., that an executive will hear your concept and announce it's the best he's heard. Short of that? Here are tangible benefits to be gained from attending a pitch event.

- Expanding your industry network — Pitch events provide a great opportunity for meeting industry executives. The single most valuable thing you can get from a pitch event is an industry executive saying, "That sounds interesting; I'd love to read that." Even if the executive ultimately passes on the script, you just added a valuable name to your network.

- Face time with targeted executives — Some executives or companies who might be ideal for your material or brand are often impossible to crack. Check out the executive roster. If the executive or his company is attending the pitch event, it might provide the perfect opportunity to connect with them.

- Useful classes and panels — Many a pitch event is part of a larger conference to which, as a participant, you gain access. Check out the panels and classes, and select those of interest. There is always something new you can learn!

**Top Five Pitch Event No-No's**

Below is a list of five things you should never ever do at a pitch event:

- Lead with your neurosis. — Nobody cares if you're about to go broke. If you've been knocking at the industry's door for years waiting for your shot. This is business. Keep it professional.

- Come unprepared. — If you signed up for pitches, the onus is on you to know who's on the other side of the desk. Make sure you know not only their names but also what they've done in the past, so that there's clarity about why you're pitching to them.

- Talk about your piles of brilliant work. — If you truly believe that you have eighteen scripts that are pure genius, the executive listening will assume the following: 1) You don't have the ability to discern good from bad, or 2) It's your personality that's the problem. Neither assertion will work in your favor.

- Extend a clammy hand. — Nervousness can be off-putting in the most subtle ways.

- Pitch to a trend. — Never ever present executives with the pitch you think they want to hear. You will not have the work to back it up, and they will assume that you're not a true storyteller.

**Leave-Behinds and Bring-Alongs**

Short of one-sheets, executives will rarely accept materials at a pitch event. No full-length screenplays, treatments, or synopses. Want to bring a costume that will illustrate what your protagonist will be wearing throughout the movie? Have a soundtrack already constructed that you want to play? Put together a chart illustrating why your project can be expected to perform? Or worse, you wrote a song about the movie, which you'd like to perform? DON'T.

You may think that I'm joking. But, having been in these rooms and shared post-event drinks with executives, I can tell you that stories of the odd, weird, and eccentric pitches will be repeated for years behind closed doors as anecdotes. Regretfully, this will not help you get your script read, optioned, or sold.

## Online Pitch Services

The popularity of pitch events gave birth to pitch-driven services. While each operates with a slightly different angle, these services offer a hyper-targeted opportunity to present your work to one of the many agents, managers, and development or production executives secured on the receiving end.

Of the myriad services out there, here are a few I recommend:

- Virtual Pitchfest — Word of VPF came to me from a client who found his way to CAA using the service. Run by David Zuckerman, the service invites you to submit a hyper-targeted pitch letter to one of the many executives in VPF's stable of industry professionals. While finding success here does require that you get busy with your pitch letter wordcraft, scribes using this site have gotten deals and secured representation.

- Greenlight My Movie — Closer to the pitch event concept, this online service invites writers and directors to submit an on-camera pitch to GMM's stable of executives. This service provides pitch recipients with a complete experience — within seconds they are able to identify whether you are someone with whom they'd want to work. This service has not only helped filmmakers find outlets for their material, but it has also garnered representation and secured deals.

Whatever method, get yourself out there. Use the opportunities the industry offers to pave those inroads, build your network, and carve those all-important relationships. This is all part of what it takes to get your material read. Which, as I've said in many different ways now, is a critical component for your success.

Chapter Nineteen

# REPRESENTATION

Every unrepresented writer I come in contact with wants to know: how do I get an agent or a manager?

Raw talent and potential are rarely enough to attract seasoned representation. With countless unrepresented writers knocking on representation's doors, it is important to know the ground rules and expectations in the representation game, while understanding how to become the sort of client — produced or just starting out — that agents and managers want to represent.

## All I Need Is an Agent

Having an agent sounds great. Someone who would work tirelessly on your behalf, getting you in front of the right people and putting your material in the right hands. You will write. They will work...

If only it were as simple as that.

### *The 90-10 Split*

As compensation, agents collect 10% of all writing-related fees they secure for their clients. Hence, the term "ten percenters," which is used not only for agents, but also for managers.

Never pay an agent out of pocket. Agents do not work on retainer; they work on spec. They invest their time and energy in you in the belief that your talent will secure financial rewards down the road for you and for them.

A seasoned literary agent working in TV once told me, "I only collect ten percent of the money, so I only do ten percent of the work."

By all accounts, the work that goes into building a screenwriting career amounts to a lot more than 10% of the work. This is where agents (and managers) will look for you to continue to network, create opportunities, and cultivate relationships.

For their 10%, agents are expected to help facilitate a script sale, option, or writing agreement, procure work, and put the deal in place. They will doggedly pursue funds due to you at various milestones of the contract, and ensure that you are fairly and promptly compensated for your work.

Your 10% covers not only the services of your agent and the team around him, but also the agency's collection department, as well as other administrative services associated with getting your work out into the marketplace.

### When Will You Need an Agent?

You need an agent when you have a superior screenplay ready to sell. It's as simple as that. Your agent will be best utilized when there is a contract to secure and a transaction to be made. While your agent will aim to get your screenplay or TV pilot into the right hands, much of their efforts go into securing paying work for their list of clients. They are not there to give notes (though some do) or hold your hand. An agent is at his best when he's allowed to facilitate an introduction, put deal points in place, paper the deal, then move on to the next.

### What Will an Agent Do for You?

An agent will help facilitate the sale of your work or otherwise procure work on your behalf utilizing your writing services. Armed with a strong screenplay, agents will do all they can to send the spec to executives whose interest might be piqued by the work. Even if the material doesn't lead to an immediate or even eventual sale, they will use it to open doors on your behalf, setting up meetings wherever they can. My hardworking friend Marissa Jo Cerar, whose screenplay *Conviction* landed her on 2012's The Black List, was introduced to many an industry company through her ICM agents. Her representation sent her material far and wide, eventually getting her staffed on a TV show.

"Generals" are meetings to which you are invited not to discuss any particular screenplay, but rather you, the brand. There is no faster way for a production entity to identify whether they might want to work with you some day. When the day comes, your agent will paper the deal (i.e., iron out all details of the contract), negotiate on your behalf, and collect payments.

As your name builds and your career grows, your agent will not only be busy sending out any new specs you might have, but will also be on the receiving end of industry calls inviting you to pitch your "take" for open writing assignments or potential rewrite jobs.

### Making the Most of the Writer/Agent Relationship

Securing the services of an agent doesn't give you license to rest on your laurels and see what manifests. In order to stay front-of-mind with your agent, you must continuously and dependably produce material that your agent can sell. As a client, you will not only be competing with other screenplays in the marketplace, but also with other writers on your agent's roster for his attention and enthusiasm.

Signing with representation typically comes on the heels of a successful script. You will then have to write an effective follow-up script that will successfully solidify your voice and extend your brand. Delivering a subpar follow-up script is certain to raise doubts in the mind of your agent. Did he make a mistake? Can you do it, successfully, again? You know the saying "Keeping an A is tougher than getting an A"? While agents do not drop their clients without reason, their enthusiasm can reduce, and fast.

In order to make the most of your relationship with your agent, make sure to deliver consistent work in a timely fashion. Train your agent to expect a new, stellar, vetted piece from you every four to six months, and deliver it like clockwork. That way, each one of your screenplays will solidify the confidence built with the last, and your timely delivery will identify you as one able to deliver consistently for the marketplace.

*The Dangers of Big Agencies*

When asked, most writers would prefer getting represented by one of the big agencies, namely CAA, ICM, UTA, Resolution, or WME. Why wouldn't you want your agent to be part of the biggest representation companies? While I have nothing against big agencies, they may not be suitable for new writers just breaking into the industry. Here are a few reasons why a big agency may not be right in the early stages of your career:

- You are an unknown commodity — As a new writer, you will join the long list of your agent's known entities, ones whose names are more established, who previously generated revenues for the company. Sure, initially your agent will do what he can to get your screenplay to as many relevant executives as he can. But ask yourself: if you had the choice of putting effort toward someone who already got you paid, versus someone who may or may not generate income one day, who would you work for first?

- Incoming vs. Outgoing — While new writers require that lots of outgoing calls be made by their representation to help build their name and brand, agents receive incoming calls and inquiries on behalf of their established, working clients every day. As a rule, incoming calls are top priority for every agent working in the literary world.

- Overhead — Big agents are housed in big buildings. With big expense accounts, and a big support staff. Their first order of business is generating revenue for their company. And securing work for their A-list talent and working writers is the fastest way to get there. That is simply how the big-agency business model works.

*Getting Hip-Pocketed*

"Getting hip-pocketed," or having a "hip pocket arrangement" refers to a somewhat favorable, and slightly limbo-like state for writers seeking to secure representation. Having a hip-pocket arrangement means that you are not on the agent's official roster, but you do have the agent's interest. As long as you continue to produce stellar, marketable work, he will do what he can (and what time allows) to help your case, with the aim of graduating you from hip pocket to official roster some day.

**Note:** If you have a hip-pocket arrangement with Agent X, who's done work on your behalf, don't sign with Agent Y without discussing it with Agent X. Agent X didn't do all that hard work to see you go work with someone else. It's one thing if Agent X doesn't want to put you on his roster. But if he's done the work, produced results, and wants to bring you into his stable, walking away without warning will reflect badly on your still-growing brand.

### Or Maybe a Manager's Better...

Originally, managers emerged from the agency world to work under a more attention-driven business model. This is, effectively, what Jerry Maguire was advocating in his famous mission statement: Fewer clients. More attention. Wrapped up in the trusted 10%.

Many working writers have both an agent and a manager: an agent to facilitate and paper the deal, a manager to help develop their career. While agents often represent dozens of writers, most managers focus on a smaller stable. Many represent only fifteen to twenty-five clients, while junior managers sport anything from five to fifteen writers on their list. While some of the larger management companies now operate more similarly to agencies, complete with large client rosters and extensive overhead, single-person and boutique management firms often operate out of their homes or moderate offices, keeping a close eye on overhead. Agency employees often receive a compensation package that is part salary, part commission; managers, on the other hand, work on commission alone until they become part of a larger firm.

### The Benefits of a Manager

Working with a good manager ordinarily allows ample time for material development before financial expectations are had. While development time is by no means infinite, many see building the right runway for their clients an integral part of their work.

Because managers work on commission alone, they often have no boss but themselves. They have no quotas to meet (specifically when running their own shop), and their success or failure lies in the sales they make. Therefore, they have a bit more leeway when operating purely on faith.

### How Will a Literary Manager Help You?

Due to their moderate client rosters, many managers do extensive work with clients prior to sale. Whether advising on creative development or suggesting a writers' group or events to attend, managers have a vested interest in setting their clients up for long-term success.

While many writers will be represented by different agencies in the span of their careers, the writer-manager relationship should be long lasting. Because of the extensive development work managers do with their clients on the front end, return of investment is expected in the long term, when the writer's career takes off and pays ongoing dividends. Manager Daniel Vang, currently at renowned boutique management company Benderspink, had a writer develop three different spec scripts *after* he signed her, until he was certain that she had one strong enough to assure success. This took time, thought, and close attention to the writer's potential career trajectory and brand.

### Agents vs. Managers: The Differences

While often working in similar ways, there are some differences between agents and managers of which to be aware:

Agents, and agencies, are licensed. Managers, and management companies, are not.

Agents are legally allowed to procure work for their clients. Though petitions have been filed to change this, at the time of this writing, managers technically are not.

This is a business of introductions. Of who you know. And most reputable managers are just as apt at setting up introductions for their clients as are agents. When a writer starts out with a manager, it's often the manager who makes the all-important introduction to an agent once the material is ready to sell.

In lieu of an agent, some managers turn to entertainment lawyers to paper a deal on their client's behalf.

While you should not expect extensive notes from an agent (at best, you will likely get those from assistants or readers working for them), a manager will likely read your scripts and give you notes on multiple drafts, so long as you have his interest. That said, both agents and managers are capable of dismissing a script with a single sentence: "This is not for me," or " I don't get it." In such a case, you will likely be on the bubble with both, until you are able to deliver work that they are once again excited for.

### What Your Manager Will Expect from You

Your manager will expect you to write. Write well. Write fast. Come up with great ideas; many will expect you to deliver a certain number of new ideas on a regular basis.

While some managers expect you to consistently hobnob and build your network, others (like manager Dallas Sonnier who told me that his writers don't need to take a million meetings and are better off staying home and writing) will urge you to focus on craft.

Most every manager out there will expect you to home in on and extend your brand. This way, with each new script, you will give them something they can promote to your established fan base. In keeping your managers excited about you, market-ready content is key.

### Making the Most of the Writer/Manager Relationship

To make the most of your relationship with your manager, questions must be asked and problems should be handled head-on. You want your manager responding to you, providing you with input, helping you along. Because your long-term career growth is dependent on agreed-upon strategy, don't be afraid to ask questions that will help inform your decisions. Questions like, "What should I be writing next?" or "Is there someone I should be trying to meet?" are generally well received. It doesn't mean that your manager should be making all the decisions, but rather advising you on how you move forward.

On the flip side, if you ask your manager how to move forward or which of your projects you should pursue, take that advice seriously. Receiving guidance but proceeding in a different direction communicates that while you appreciate your manager's opinion, it's not necessarily considered.

As with an agent, you want to supply your manager with new, exciting work on a regular basis. Make sure your work is vetted and looked at by others before you turn it in — most managers don't have the bandwidth to help you refine your work from early drafts; you want to consistently deliver work strong enough to impress.

### *The Danger of Off-the-Radar Management*

Is it better to be represented by an off-the-radar manager than not be represented at all?

Managers are useful to the writers they represent due to their established connections and reputation in the industry, which can help open doors and put the writers they represent in positions instrumental for success. Managers without these valuable connections can do little to move your career forward.

When considering whether a manager is worthwhile, do your research, and seek evidence of their track record. One great resource is *The Scoggins Report*. Look at the previous year's spec sales report, and find how many specs — if any — a particular manager or his company sold. Sure, everyone would love to have the likes of super-manager Brooklyn Weaver blowing up their phone. But short of that, make sure that the management you're talking to is industry-connected, and getting spec scripts out into the marketplace.

Chapter Twenty

# DOING THE HARD WORK YOURSELF

If chutzpah is your thing, why not do it yourself?

Manager Jewerl Ross once told a roomful of writers eager to know how they could get a manager, "Why do you need a manager? At the outset of your career, what can I do for you that you can't do for yourself?" The subtext? Take the reins and pave meaningful inroads into the industry marketplace.

## Approaching Development and Production Executives

At the end of the day, representation, a strong pitch, or even a Nicholl win do not a movie or a TV show make (though they certainly help!). The fate of a project, and its trajectory going from script to screen, relies entirely on interest from development and production executives as they consider material for their ever-evolving slates. Finding effective ways to get them excited about your work is a huge step for building your long-term screenwriting success.

### *Do Your Research for the Targeted Approach*

While some development and production executives are more approachable for writers, others, specifically those who have a high-profile production company (such as Alcon Entertainment or Relativity Media), studio deals (think Bad Robot), or are part of the studios themselves, will be harder to approach, and will not accept material from an unknown writer unsolicited.

To be clear, here we are exploring the direct route. Not the utilization of pitch events that allow opportunities to network, or going through services such as Greenlight My Movie or Virtual Pitchfest.

When going for the direct route, it's important to consider *whom* you target, rather than *how many* companies are in your sites. If you approach a dozen companies who have some clout but are not studio affiliated, you will likely have a significantly higher chance for success than if you approached a hundred studio and network executives, who will rarely (and by rarely I mean never) accept material that is not from a known source, a name writer, or already packaged.

When you consider approaching producers and development executives, look not only at whether they have current projects on their individual résumé or company slates, but also whether they do projects like yours. Ask yourself (and answer objectively): Is my material in line with the projects they already do? Is it different enough than what they've done before?

While everyone with an action script would love to approach Jerry Bruckheimer's company, this particular shop, now part of Disney, will likely not read work that came from an unknown source. You insist that Bruckheimer is your ultimate home? Research their slate of recent releases, and see what other production companies were involved. Poking through you will find that on *The Sorcerer's Apprentice* Saturn Films, Nicolas Cage's shingle, was also listed as a production company. This company may not be receiving blind submissions either, but with a smaller shop and a hyper-targeted query, you will stand a better chance for success than you would with Bruckheimer.

### *Every Buyer Has a Buyer: Understanding the Strategic Approach*

When approaching a production company with your material, it's important to remember that they have their own industry brand, on which their prominence is based. Buyers come to them again and again based on the material they've successfully produced in the past. Therefore, it's important to know the genre preference and historical slate of any company you're approaching in order to determine whether there's a possibility that your material would be a match.

Take Tapestry Films, which rose to glory on the heels of such comedic triumphs as *The Wedding Planner*, *Van Wilder*, and *Wedding Crashers*.

Approach them with the next *Prometheus* and they likely won't know what to do with it. Their reputation was built delivering comedies, which is what both distribution companies and studios now seek from them.

Over time, a company may venture into new genres, but likely only when involving players (i.e., screenwriters, director, and talent) with an established reputation. This was just the case with Tapestry Films, who dove head first into straight-drama/Academy Award–contender territory with *Pay It Forward*. The talent attached: Kevin Spacey and Helen Hunt (both Academy Award winners) in the lead roles, and Mimi Leder in the director's chair.

### Development and Creative Executives: What Do They Do?

In the new millennium most self-respecting production companies have a development department powered by well-connected development personnel. In lieu of those? Enter the creative executive.

The job of a development or creative executive may sound simple: find superior material that meshes with the company's brand, and develop it to attract talent, ultimately getting it to a stage where it can be financed and made. Build relationships with writers and directors of note. Maintain strong relationships with representation and production executives. Put together effective attachments (actors and director of name) for projects.

Think this is simple? Think again.

Unless they're working for, say, Imagine Entertainment, development executives have to compete to be on the receiving end of hot material and hot pitches every day. Everyone wants "in" on the hot script. Development personnel and creative executives (also known as CE's) take meetings with writers and directors, listening to pitches every day. They read — voraciously — most everything they can. To find the next hot director, they watch shorts and movies en masse. Additionally, they cultivate relationships with talent agents and managers, in the hopes of attracting high-value actors and directors for any projects they might be developing in-house themselves.

## Producers and Production Executives: What Are Their Jobs?

If, on a movie set, the director is the captain of the ship, the producer is the one responsible for building the ship, equipping, and manning it, as well as keeping it on course for the journey ahead.

Independent producers such as Tracey Becker, who found the two-act play *The Man Who Was Peter Pan* and developed it into the Academy Award–nominated *Finding Neverland*, often get involved in the early stages of material development and take projects all the way through fundraising, production, and even distribution sales. They will bring on the director, raise the money, identify the location, and decide what funds are spent where. Long after a film is done shooting, they will be engaged in the postproduction world. Most directors do not have final cut (the final assembly of footage that ends up on the big screen). Instead, they present their director's cut, then leave the project in the producer's hands. The producer not only oversees editorial changes, but also supervises sound mix, picture finishing, special effects, and music.

Production executives are responsible for making key decisions on behalf of their company (such as how much budget should be spent and where, where the film or TV show is to be shot, etc.), find key incentives and deals that will help bring the project in within budget, while reviewing dailies (footage produced on set) every day to keep a close eye on the quality of the material produced.

As part of their job, production executives oversee the work of the on-set producer, line producer, or production manager. The on-set producer will hear concerns when dailies come back showing that material is not lit properly or that material is not being shot at the pace expected and that the production is falling behind schedule. If the production executive feels that the on-set producer is ineffective, he may replace the individual or bring in support. When a project goes over-budget or over-schedule, it's the producer whom the money people and the production executives will be looking to.

Chapter Twenty-One

# ONGOING MARKETING EFFORTS
# FOR YOUR SCREENPLAY AND BRAND

It's the mission of any business to market itself in order to get word out about what it does. The customary definition of marketing is:

*"The action or business of promoting and selling products and services."*

For screenwriters, specs scripts — be they feature or pilot — are your products, and screenwriting itself the service you provide. In this context, marketing relates to any outgoing effort to bring your work and skill to the right people's attention. It can range from ongoing networking efforts, all the way to deliberate emails informing your network that you just finished a new screenplay or placed in a high-value contest.

## The Benefits of Ongoing Marketing Efforts

Consistent marketing efforts take you from the writer who just showed up on the scene, or a fly-by-night who happened to win a single screenwriting contest, to one who is deliberately working toward his screenwriting career. Displaying that you are consistently delivering quality material, entering contests, and pursuing the appropriate, recognizable avenues for success, confirms not only that you're talented and prolific, but also that you understand how the industry works.

Professionals want to work with other professionals; if you communicate valuable, relevant information on an ongoing basis and reinforce the value of your work, sooner or later, and so long as it's real, you may just pique their interest.

Remember, marketing, in this instance, does not mean sending out an email blast or taking out a billboard. It means pursuing ongoing efforts in which you can communicate the progress you've made and the success you've accumulated for your products. Because the industry is a casual social environment, efforts that can fall under the marketing header may include everything from going to an industry event and connecting with new industry executives to sending targeted emails touting the latest developments to your industry network.

### Creating Your Own Marketing Opportunities

For screenwriters, marketing opportunities are not going to create themselves. It takes deliberate planning to make sure that you have ongoing reasons to market yourself.

Marketing reasons can include finishing and vetting a screenplay. Send a quick email to your professional network, letting them know that you've just completed a screenplay you're very excited about. In the email, include the material's title, genre, and logline, and invite the recipient to have a read. You submitted your screenplay for coverage and it got a "Consider"? Even better. If the coverage comes from a renowned industry source, you can use a short, effective quote. Make sure the email is personal, using their name rather than "Dear Sir" or "Dear Mrs." Remind your recipients where you've met, or check in on how they've been; this is, after all, relationship building.

No response? A few months later, try again.

This time you've won or placed in a high-value screenwriting contest. You send an email humbly touting your victory. Put it in the subject line — make sure it can't be missed. Someone else just endorsed your talent and you want to make sure the person on the receiving end knows this.

Not native to Los Angeles? Plan an annual or biannual trip to LA. Send an email to your industry contacts in advance: *I'm coming to Los Angeles for a series of professional meetings, and would love to buy you a cup of coffee if you are available.*

They say yes? Don't ask them for anything. Instead, pick their brains, find out what sort of material they're looking for or what sort of writers they like to work with. If they feel you're genuine, they will extend a helping hand.

## Cashing In on Every Win, No Matter How Small or Big

On too many occasions, I run into writers who did not capitalize on a "win" because it wasn't the win they wanted; they placed as finalist in a contest, but did not ultimately win. They got a "Consider" coverage from one of the reputable coverage services, but not a "Recommend."

While it is important that you don't "oversell" news that doesn't mean much to anyone except for you (i.e., placing as a quarterfinalist in an irrelevant contest), make sure to get news of value out there. A production company wants to option your material? *Script* magazine would like to interview you about your recent accomplishments? An established actor is participating in a reading of your work? All of those, and many more, are valid reasons to market yourself.

Chapter Twenty-Two

# WHAT ELSE DO YOU HAVE?

Oh, those magical words.

Some writers hate hearing them: it means the script at hand did not stimulate immediate interest. And while it is true for the work, it is the opposite for the brand. It means that something about the writer or the work has piqued the reader's interest, inspiring him to explore whether the writer has other work that would be more suitable, marketable, or plain interesting for him. Play your cards right, and you may just turn this initial interest into a long-standing relationship which could, in time, pay dividends.

This seemingly simple question comes to answer a myriad of things for the listening executive:

- Do you have more than one script in you? — Or is this the best you've got? Executives want to know that you are able to develop other material that might be of interest.

- Are you developing new work, or resting on your laurels? — Both representation and development executives are looking to build relationships with prolific brands. If you've got one script and nothing else, you will inevitably be of lesser interest to them as far as the long term is concerned.

## Parallel Idea Development

Because of the "What else do you have?" question, it is of utmost importance that you are always thinking creatively. Idea development is integral to the work of a screenwriter — in fact, many managers ask their writers to deliver a set number of new ideas every month, and I too work with my writers to encourage such creative development.

In order to have fresh, exciting ideas to share in prospective meetings and casual encounters, get in the habit of cultivating your new ideas while toiling away on any given screenplay. Create a repository for your ideas, be it a physical drawer or a file on your computer, one you can go to again and again, revisit, and explore when it's time to consider your next work.

## Identifying Your Next Script

When deciding on your next script, ask yourself: "What have I done great in my last screenplay? How do I take the strengths displayed, and push them further, in this format or another, in a way that would complement my body of work?"

Don't try to figure out what the industry is looking for, or chase the trends; your next screenplay should be native to your unique creative vision, effectively solidifying and extending your brand. This doesn't mean repeating subjects or replicating characters; rather, it's about confirming your dominance in a particular genre, which will give you the best chance to establish yourself as an expert.

Chapter Twenty-Three

# PRACTICAL GUIDELINES
# FOR SUBMISSION AND FOLLOW-UPS

Finally! You got that all-important bite: a request to read your script. Whether the request came through a pitch event, an online pitching service, a contest win, or an industry contact, doesn't matter. The point is... congratulations! Your hard work is paying off.

Let's examine etiquette and expectations when getting your material out there.

### Sending Your Script Out for Reads

When you send your script out, the draft you send better be THE draft. The one you got notes on, the one you had professionally beaten up in order to make it the best script it can be.

There are no redos here. The last thing you want is to realize a week after you've sent it that the draft is a disaster, only to email the recipient saying, "Oops! I actually need to pull the draft back." While this is better than having them read a bad draft, hate it, and never want to hear from you again, it's still highly unprofessional. Without any question or doubt, the draft you send out should be THE ONE.

When you send a script in for an executive or a potential representative to read, make sure you've gone meticulously through the material to eliminate any typos that might have been missed. Industry folks hate typos; some say that if you can't be bothered to send them a clean script, they can't be bothered to read. So spend the extra time, or give it to a friend with a good eye. You don't want to have your script dismissed on a technicality.

Here are some scheduling suggestions for sending in your script:

- Never email your script in on a Monday. — Mondays are busy days in the industry. Your material will be lost in all the activity.

- Don't email your material in the middle of the night. — By the time the executive gets to the office, there will be a million emails that came in the morning and trumped it.

- End of day Friday (or the weekend in general) is not the time to email in your script. — Unless he's waiting for it, your targeted executive will likely forget about it by the time the new week begins.

A few title page guidelines:

- You're a writer, not a production company. — If you've established a production company, your title page is not the page to display it. You're sending the material as a writer — having a production company on the title page will only confuse things.

- Leave "An Original Screenplay By" out of it. — Unless credit is due to someone else (i.e., based on a true story, a book, a short story, etc.), the assumption is that the material is original.

- Forget the lyrics, the poetry, the quotes. — Don't waste pages on your favorite quotes, on the reason why this story is important, on song lyrics that somehow apply. Get us into the script as quickly as you can, without giving the reader any reason to set it aside.

Once the script is ready to send, include a note reminding the executive — if you've not been in ongoing communication — where you've met. Include a quick logline for the material, and sign off by thanking the recipient in advance for his time and consideration.

## The Pitch Event Follow-Up

Got a request for material at a pitch event? Great! You have no time to waste.

If the executive asked to see material that you told him was complete, you have two to three weeks to get it to him. Better, of course, if you get it to him faster. Anything more than three weeks gives you away as a novice who pitched material that wasn't ready to share. Wait a month or two, and the executive will have lost interest. If the material was completed but you failed to send it, you didn't give his request the importance it deserved.

If the material needs one last read and will then be ready to send, get it into the right hands, and FAST. Rush coverage, get notes, and work in any rewrites you want before you've exceeded the three-week time frame. When you send the script, make sure to remind the executive where you met, that he requested the screenplay, and include the logline that piqued his interest.

If the executive expressed interest in an idea you told him you were currently working on, send him an email after the event and thank him. Once again, remind him of the event where you met, as well as of the logline that piqued his interest. Tell him you will be working hard on the idea in the coming weeks and months, and will be in touch again when you have material ready to share. When the screenplay's been completed, vetted, and rewritten to perfection (hopefully within a four to six month time frame), drop him an email letting him know that you've competed the screenplay, and offer to send it.

## The All-Important (and Ongoing) Follow-Ups

Once your screenplay has been requested and sent, don't abandon it! While most executives will make their best efforts to review any solicited material, if they are stretched too thin, it may get swallowed up in their virtual reading piles.

Follow up within three weeks of the date the script was sent with a short, concise email thanking the executive again for his interest, and confirming that he received your material. Three more weeks pass and no word? It's time for another follow-up. Remind the executive where you met or under which circumstance he requested your screenplay, and thank him in advance for his time. Still nothing? Follow up with two more quick emails, in two-week intervals. No answer? Regretfully, that is an answer right there. Either the executive read it and did not respond, or he simply did not have the time to read.

The important thing is that you followed up. When your next screenplay is ready, reach out to the executive again and invite him to take a look at your new work. He may have more availability then.

## What Does It Mean?
## Decoding Hollywood's Silent Messages and Subtexts

Both working writers and aspiring writers often complain that they are getting mixed messages, or no communication at all, from industry executives. A script was requested, but no feedback given one way or another. A meeting was suggested, but you can't get anyone on the phone to set a date.

Just because an industry executive is not answering your email or returning your call, does not mean he's not sending you a message. As *Real Time with Bill Maher* writer Chris Kelly once put it: "In Hollywood, 'No' is silence over time... It's the call you don't get."

Knowing things are not always communicated directly, let's explore the subtext:

- The Silent Treatment — You sent in a script, followed up, but have not been told whether the script is of interest? If more than eight to ten weeks have passed and you've been following up consistently without receiving word, you got your answer: the script is not of interest.

- "The material is not right for us at this time." — The executive did not respond to the work. However, you may just become the next John August, and if you do, that's one bridge the executive doesn't want to burn.

- "I really liked the script but… " — While any compliments may be true, the material was not enough for the executive to jump in. Take it with a grain of salt and enjoy it for what it's worth.

- "Keep us posted about your next screenplay." — Open door alert! Sure, the executive did not respond as you had hoped, but possibly liked your voice nonetheless. Even if it's just out of politeness, take whatever you can get.

When things do happen, they tend to happen fast. You will be invited to a meeting, told to stand by for a conference call, or get the heads-up about forthcoming paperwork. One thing is for sure: you will know, beyond a shadow of a doubt, when it's a real, firm "Yes."

### Turning a "No" into a Next Step

Nobody wants to hear a "No," silent or otherwise. But if you've been doing this long enough, you know that it's not about the hundreds of no's you are going to hear — it's about finally getting that "YES"!

In order to make this happen, keep working every relationship, every connection, until you get there.

Got a "Pass" from an executive, an agent, or manager? Send him a letter or an email, thank him for taking the time to read, and let him know that you are currently working on other material, which you would love to share once it's ready.

Without coming off as desperate, do what you can to keep the door open and the conversation going. Taking rejection well may just allow you the opportunity for success someday. No matter what, remember this: every writer working today heard more than a few "No's" along the way!

Chapter Twenty-Four

# FACING THE MUSIC:
# WHEN THINGS DON'T GO YOUR WAY

This is the part no one wants to hear. The realization that despite all the hard work, things just didn't go as planned: You've spent the last six to twelve months peddling the same script. You've gotten it coverage. Confirmed that it's worthy of a "Consider." Made all the right moves, contacted all the right people, but still... The momentum everyone promised isn't there.

Time to stop, catch your breath, and assess where you are, what might have gone wrong, and what to do next.

### How to Recognize When Your Screenplay Is Not Working

Here are some of the inevitable signs that your screenplay is not performing well:

- You entered a number of contests but never placed. — If you entered your screenplay into four to five screenwriting contests but never reached the finalists' circle, your script is not being received as you intended. If it were, someone somewhere would have pushed it ahead.

- No bites from management. — You went through the pitch events, utilized online introduction services, and made the most of your network, but even though you've gotten your screenplay into the hands of a number of managers, every single one was a "Pass." They had no interest in talking to you. The screenplay did not resonate.

- Production companies are not showing interest. — You've gotten your screenplay into a number of qualified hands, but no one is showing interest. You may, at best, have gotten something saying "Don't hesitate to let us know when you have something else," but otherwise... No interest.

Let's be abundantly clear: it SUCKS. It sucks that, despite all the hard work, that's the result you get. It's hard, and it hurts. But there is one thing to remember: you build a screenwriting career on the strength of the brand, not the merit of one script. Therefore, for the sake of your screenwriting career, it's time to assess your options, and decide what to do next.

## The Writing Is on the Wall: Course Correcting

If you sent your screenplay to contests and executives without getting professional feedback first, this is the time to investigate where your screenplay may have gone awry. While you won't be able to resubmit your work to producers, development executives, agents, and managers who have already passed, it's important that you are able to identify, for the sake of your next script, where the last one failed.

The biggest mistake many writers make is assuming industry executives "just didn't get it." Folks in the industry have been doing this for a long time. They know how to find the projects that are right for them and hold potential for the marketplace. If it's a career you're looking to build, look to the script, the genre, and the subject matter objectively to understand where it failed. It's imperative that you learn from each of your screenplays, whether they succeeded or failed. Reflections on the performance of your work can help isolate weaknesses and identify strengths. After all, the job of a screenwriter is to convey your vision to the reader in a powerful and compelling way. If your screenplay failed to do this, or tackled a genre or subject matter that has proven difficult to sell, it's important that you turn to other professionals to help you understand past mistakes, if only so that you don't end up in this situation again.

### Reassessing, Re-Strategizing, Adjusting, and Moving Ahead

A time comes in every prolific screenwriter's journey when he realizes that a particular script didn't generate the reaction he believed it deserved.

The good news? This happens to everyone. If after many rejections you've suddenly realized an elegant and pivotal shift that will finally push the material to that elusive next level, congratulations! However, you won't be able to send it back to executives, managers, and agents who already passed. Changing the screenplay's title and resubmitting it to the same industry executives or company — unless invited to do so — is a no-no.

Most importantly, if you realize that your best course of action might be to move on to your next screenplay, it's important that you do the following:

- Mourn whatever did not go your way. — You've worked hard, and no matter the reasoning, it's disappointing.

- Try to examine, objectively, why the screenplay was not received as you expected. — No matter how disappointing, every situation allows an opportunity to learn.

- Strategically decide what your brand would most benefit from as far as your next screenplay. — Approach it with purpose, deliberation, and clarity as to how in six to eight months your next project will help you make a case for your brand.

Chapter Twenty-Five

# YOUR SCREENWRITING CAREER: LOOKING AHEAD

A wise man once said, "Hope for the best, prepare for the worst." The reality is that, in the world of screenwriting, success will likely be somewhere in between.

Everyone wants to sell his spec screenplay for a million bucks, or to become a showrunner his first time out of the gate. But for many a screenwriter, building a screenwriting career is a long, expertly executed marathon at the end of which they get to write for a living, develop exciting work, make powerful connections, and continue to solidify and extend their voices over many years and many screenplays.

With any luck, in time you will become one of them. Here's a look at some of the details, intricacies, and possibilities that may lie ahead.

## The Complexities of Screenplay Options

While most any writer would love to sell a screenplay right off the bat, unless you find yourself in a bidding situation, in which multiple producing entities and/or studios are vying to secure exclusive rights to your work, it is customary for a production entity to request an option period prior to purchasing a screenplay. An option period will allow the production entity to take the screenplay out for a proverbial spin and see what sort of interest it garners from talent and financing before making a full financial commitment.

Screenplay options come in all shapes and sizes. In order for an option to be legal, money has to change hands. Enter the "dollar option," a transaction involving legal tender and thereby legal and valid. Don't be surprised if this is the offer you receive when optioning a screenplay the first or even fifth time out — the producing entity will invest a lot more in legal fees, time, and effort into the project. While not every option concludes with a script purchase, and not every script purchase leads to a produced film or television show, it is, for many, the first and most important step.

Make sure these points are clarified when you're considering a script option:

- What is the term of the option? — Options may run from forty-five days to twenty-four months. Be sure that the paperwork you are provided is clear about the production company's rights for renewal, as well as under which circumstances the rights to the material revert back to you.

- Does the option spell out compensation in case of sale? — Many option agreements spell out a "floor and ceiling" expectation for your compensation should the script be purchased.

- Will rewrite fees be paid if rewrites are required? — Or are you expected to deliver rewrites without additional pay?

If you don't have an agent or a manager when you reach this all-important milestone, hire an established entertainment lawyer to review the paperwork on your behalf.

## Elements and Attachments

When a production entity becomes interested in your material and potentially options or even buys it, the first thing it will do once any additional development work is completed is attach elements of value to the material.

Elements are defined as known entities, such as actors or a director, who have a proven and current box-office track record, and therefore bring known value to the package for your project. At this stage, casting directors and development executives will become involved, sifting through lists of talent that would be "bankable," available, and suitable for the material. Many A-list actors are often booked months and years in advance; the producing entity will aim to deliver the material based on a specific schedule, and will attach elements based on that.

Often, independent producers will seek to bring on board elements against which the movie's financing will be secured. Many an independent project (and a few studio projects too) are cast-dependent, i.e., the funding will only be given once approved actors have committed to the project. Note that when bringing elements to a project, executives will focus on household names with current successes at the box office.

### Writers Lists

You can't talk your way onto a writers list. The only way to make a case for yourself is with your work.

Writers lists are kept by every development department of every production company and studio out there. When one of its executives reads something from a writer whose voice he likes, that writer may be added to the list under an appropriate category. Such categories may include "great with dialogue" or "original comedy voice" or "good for polish."

It is customary for many production companies to develop material in house — material based on an internal concept with a chosen writer. The concept may come from anything and everything: a magazine article, a blog post, something they saw on the street, which gave birth to a cinematic concept. Once the department has committed to the concept, executives will call on writers to pitch their "take" and make their case to be chosen for the development of the material. That's when favorite scripts and writers lists are pulled out. The executives usually invite a number of writers to pitch, and ultimately select the one whose skills are proven, and whose approach they are most excited about.

Other occasions when writers lists are pulled out is when a production company has a book or short story to adapt, or when it's time to polish or punch up dialogue, all part of an existing project's rewrite.

Remember this: there is no way of knowing if you've made it onto a writers list. But when you do, you'll often get invited to come in to the company for a "general," simply giving the executive(s) the opportunity to get to know you before they decide whether to bring you in for a particular project.

## Open Writing Assignments

Open writing assignments, also known as OWAs, used to be the bread and butter of many a working writer. OWAs refer to anything from a rewrite job to a writing gig developing material with a development executive.

While open writing assignments still exist in the independent world, they are not as prevalent as they used to be on the studio level. No longer are they posted on tracking boards for agents and managers to send in their best and brightest; nowadays, studios often resort to using writers already on their approved lists, ones they have likely worked with before, or whose material they purchased.

This does not mean that you can't get there! Keep churning out stellar material and developing your reputation, and soon enough you will pique the right people's interest. In time, and with the right, exceptionally executed material in hand, your career will not only have script options and sales along its path, but also lucrative writing assignments on "go" studio projects. Just keep at it, and you will get there!

# FINAL THOUGHTS

By now, I hope that my message has resonated: becoming a screenwriter in today's industry is something that has to be earned. Put in your hard work, develop your unique strategy, stick to it, and you have a good chance of seeing your dreams become reality. Keep writing, keep learning, keep building your network and extending your brand. Do it with purpose, with input, with guidance. Do it consistently and don't let up. Everyone wants in. It's the ones who treat this like a career, not a fluke or a whim, who see their screenwriting dreams come to life.

Before you put this book down, here are the last bits of advice I would like to leave with you:

## 1. Don't let time pass you by.

Time is NOT your friend. It is NOT on your side. Time is an adversary to keep your eye on. So don't waste your time.

You got a contest win? Interest? Take it, and run with it NOW. Start and finish a new script every six months. Remember, before you get represented, that's easy time. Once you're represented, your agent or manager will look to you for a stellar script every three to four months. It will be your objective to keep delivering the kind of quality content that will keep you front of mind. And if you're not yet represented? Time to get your writing habits and schedule in line.

A writer's job is to write. Keep developing ideas and new work, all the time. Do not sit on your laurels and wait to see what comes from the last screenplay you put out. Quality is balanced by quantity in this game. So it doesn't matter if you did it once. Or, worse, if you did it once five years ago. The industry wants to see you producing content ALL THE TIME.

## 2. Keep developing your craft.

For the professionals on the other side of the decision-making desk, it's important that you are an expert, a master of your craft. Writers who get noticed, who get industry pros wanting to work with them, are those who can hold an informed, opinionated conversation about the many elements and mechanisms of not only their screenplays, but other produced works. You will be expected to talk B-plots, character arcs, midpoints, dark-night-of-the-soul and plot reversals with masterful confidence.

So study up, and don't look back. Enter screenwriting programs. Become part of a writing group. Share pages. Get feedback. Watch movies. TV shows. Lots of them. Break them down. Analyze them every which way. This is a thinking man's game. Develop your craft and improve your chances of one day becoming the expert with whom industry pros want to work.

## 3. Remember: This is a marathon.

It bears repeating: screenwriting careers are rarely built on the strength of one screenplay or one contact. They're built brick by brick, screenplay atop of a great idea, a contest win atop a new representation contact.

It takes passion, determination, and dogged faith in the stories you tell to make it as a screenwriter, so hang on to them; they are precious. And rejection? That's just par for the course. It may not always be easy. Some days, and some projects, will not go the way that you'd hoped. But this is a game of tenacity, so keep on keeping on. Ask yourself: What can I accomplish? What is within my control? And against that, set a strategy constructed of realistic goals.

Look at every working writer in today's marketplace. They failed. They were rejected. There was a time when things didn't always go their way. But they stuck to it, wrote the next script, made the next contact. You never know what screenwriting success will look like. There is no unified path for screenwriters, so don't pretend to know when and how success will show up for you. Just trust that it will, and keep moving, steadily and methodically toward your goal.

This is not going to be easy, but then, things worth doing rarely are. Take what you've learned from this book, the guidance that resonated with you, and apply it to your pursuit. As long as you keep moving forward determinedly, with purpose and intention, strategically making decisions, cultivating contacts and intelligently expanding your brand, you have as good a chance as any to get there.

# ABOUT THE AUTHOR

LEE ZAHAVI JESSUP is an expert career coach working with screen-writers in the application of strategic business approach as they prepare for, emerge, and develop in the film, television, and new media space.

Growing up in multifaceted Israel, Lee got her first taste of the film world as an inquisitive eleven-year-old on her father's bustling movie set, and has been hooked ever since. Migrating to the United States at thirteen with her family, she landed her first production gig at seven-teen, only months after her early high school graduation. Stints in film production, postproduction, and film development followed, until Lee landed a business leadership role with Baseline, an entertainment data firm.

At Baseline, Lee was installed at the helm of *ScriptShark.com*, the primary destination for screenwriters seeking professional coverage on the Web. Lee spent six and a half years with the leading brand, dur-ing which business more than doubled. At ScriptShark, Lee introduced countless writers to the industry marketplace, resulting in myriad successful representation, assignment, and option relationships. She also launched a successful national seminar series in cooperation with Final Draft exploring the business side of a screenwriter's career. The seminar series was sponsored by the New York Times Company. In 2012, Lee left Baseline to work with writers exclusively.

Today, Lee provides career coaching to writers eager to approach their creative careers with deliberate strategy. Her extensive list of active clients includes Emmy- and Golden Globe–nominated scribes, WGA writers, best-selling authors, screenwriters who sold projects to major studios and production companies, writers represented by top agencies and management companies, as well as scribes just starting out and eager to adopt a business perspective from initial stages. Additionally, Lee works with companies and experts in the screenwriting space on business and brand strategies.

You can learn more about Lee's services and offerings at: *www. leejessup.com.*

# CINEMATIC STORYTELLING
## THE 100 MOST POWERFUL FILM CONVENTIONS EVERY FILMMAKER MUST KNOW

JENNIFER VAN SIJLL

## BEST SELLER

How do directors use screen direction to suggest conflict? How do screenwriters exploit film space to show change? How does editing style determine emotional response?

Many first-time writers and directors do not ask these questions. They forego the huge creative resource of the film medium, defaulting to dialog to tell their screen story. Yet most movies are carried by sound and picture. The industry's most successful writers and directors have mastered the cinematic conventions specific to the medium. They have harnessed non-dialog techniques to create some of the most cinematic moments in movie history.

This book is intended to help writers and directors more fully exploit the medium's inherent storytelling devices. It contains 100 non-dialog techniques that have been used by the industry's top writers and directors. From *Metropolis* and *Citizen Kane* to *Dead Man* and *Kill Bill*, the book illustrates — through 500 frame grabs and 75 script excerpts — how the inherent storytelling devices specific to film were exploited.

You will learn:
· How non-dialog film techniques can advance story.
· How master screenwriters exploit cinematic conventions to create powerful scenarios.

*"Cinematic Storytelling scores a direct hit in terms of concise information and perfectly chosen visuals, and it also searches out... and finds... an emotional core that many books of this nature either miss or are afraid of."*
— Kirsten Sheridan, Director, *Disco Pigs*; Co-writer, *In America*

*"Here is a uniquely fresh, accessible, and truly original contribution to the field. Jennifer van Sijll takes her readers in a wholly new direction, integrating aspects of screenwriting with all the film crafts in a way I've never before seen. It is essential reading not only for screenwriters but also for filmmakers of every stripe."*
— Prof. Richard Walter, UCLA Screenwriting Chairman

JENNIFER VAN SIJLL has taught film production, film history, and screenwriting. She is currently on the faculty at San Francisco State's Department of Cinema.

**$24.95 · 230 PAGES · ORDER NUMBER 35RLS · ISBN: 9781932907056**

# THE COFFEE BREAK SCREENWRITER
## WRITING YOUR SCRIPT TEN MINUTES AT A TIME

### PILAR ALESSANDRA

At last, leading Hollywood screenwriting instructor Pilar Alessandra shows everyone who's ever wanted to write a screenplay how to do it — without quitting their jobs or leaving their families. Packed with over sixty 10-minute writing tools, *The Coffee Break Screenwriter* keeps it focused and keeps it simple. Now, writers can make real progress on their scripts with only ten minutes of stolen time.

The writer receives guidance and tips at every stage of the often intimidating writing process with a relaxed, "ten minutes at a time" method that focuses the writer and pushes him or her forward. At each step, writers are encouraged to "Take Ten" and tackle an element of their scripts using the templates and tools provided. "What You've Accomplished" sections help writers review their progress. And "Ten Minute Lectures" distill and demystify old-school theory, allowing the writer to unblock and keep writing.

*"I had a 'first-draft paperweight' on my desk for months. With Pilar's help, my scripts have transformed from desk clutter into calling cards. I've been hired by Warner Bros., signed with ICM, and am a new member of the WGA. I can honestly say that I wouldn't be in the position I am today if it weren't for Pilar."*

> — Bill Birch, writer of *Shazam*, Warner Bros.

*"Pilar's techniques not only fine-tune your draft but serve as lessons that stick with you and make you a better writer overall. I highly recommend her if you want to take your writing to the next level!"*

> — Monica Macer, staff writer *Prison Break* and *Lost*; former creative executive Disney Studios

PILAR ALESSANDRA is the director of the Los Angeles writing program "On the Page," which has helped thousands of screenwriters write and develop their feature and television scripts. She's worked as Senior Story Analyst for DreamWorks and Radar Pictures and has trained writers at ABC/Disney, MTV/Nickelodeon, the National Screen Institute, the Los Angeles Film School, The UCLA Writers Program, and more. Her students and clients have sold to Disney, DreamWorks, Warner Brothers, and Sony and have won prestigious competitions such as the Austin Film Festival Screenplay Competition and the Nicholl Fellowship. See her website at *www.onthepage.tv*

**$24.95 · 280 PAGES · ORDER NUMBER 149RLS · ISBN 13: 9781932907803**

## SELLING YOUR STORY IN 60 SECONDS
### THE GUARANTEED WAY TO GET
### YOUR SCREENPLAY OR NOVEL READ

**MICHAEL HAUGE**

Best-selling author Michael Hauge reveals:
- · How to Design, Practice, and Present the 60-Second Pitch
- · The Cardinal Rule of Pitching
- · The 10 Key Components of a Commercial Story
- · The 8 Steps to a Powerful Pitch
- · Targeting Your Buyers
- · Securing Opportunities to Pitch
- · Pitching Templates
- · And much more, including "The Best Pitch I Ever Heard," an exclusive collection from major film executives

*"Michael Hauge's principles and methods are so well argued that the mysteries of effective screenwriting can be understood — even by directors."*

— Phillip Noyce, director, *Patriot Games, Clear and Present Danger, The Quiet American, Rabbit-Proof Fence*

*"... one of the few authentically good teachers out there. Every time I revisit my notes, I learn something new or reinforce something that I need to remember."*

— Jeff Arch, screenwriter, *Sleepless in Seattle, Iron Will*

*"Michael Hauge's method is magic — but unlike most magicians, he shows you how the trick is done."*

— William Link, screenwriter & co-creator, *Columbo; Murder, She Wrote*

*"By following the formula we learned in Michael Hauge's seminar, we got an agent, optioned our script, and now have a three-picture deal at Disney."*

— Paul Hoppe and David Henry, screenwriters

MICHAEL HAUGE is the author of *Writing Screenplays That Sell*, now in its 30th printing, and has presented his seminars and lectures to more than 30,000 writers and filmmakers. He has coached hundreds of screenwriters and producers on their screenplays and pitches, and has consulted on projects for Warner Brothers, Disney, New Line, CBS, Lifetime, Julia Roberts, Jennifer Lopez, Kirsten Dunst, and Morgan Freeman.

**$12.95 · 150 PAGES · ORDER NUMBER 64RLS · ISBN: 9781932907209**

# RIDING THE ALLIGATOR
## STRATEGIES FOR A CAREER IN SCREENPLAY WRITING
### (AND NOT GETTING EATEN)

### PEN DENSHAM

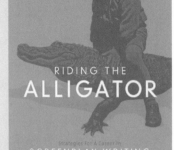

This is the first book that explores both specific screenplay writing techniques, while simultaneously imparting industry-tested strategies for carving out a successful, long term career. Pen Densham reveals his emotional philosophies and professional secrets, plus insights from his company, Trilogy Entertainment Group. Pen imparts an inspiring philosophy on choosing an artistic career and overcoming the many challenges, such as managing stress, to selling yourself and your work, to finding an agent and being true to one's nature, all while creating a lasting and satisfying career. Pen draws from his own successful self-taught approach to the industry. He speaks from a place of tremendous empathy for writers, as someone who personally identifies with their creative struggles. He believes there are many right ways to find your voice as an artist and so, going one step further, Pen has included short essays from some of Hollywood's top screenwriters, who each share their particular perspective on their art and career.

*"As a director, I cannot achieve my goals without the help of creative and courageous writers. Pen's book is unique in that it addresses the entire landscape of movie writing as a career, and most especially encourages artists who write from the heart and strive for originality."*
        — Ron Howard, director/producer/writer/actor

*"If you're thinking about writing a screenplay, do yourself a favor and hop on Pen Densham's Alligator. The ride's enlightening."*
        — Jeff Bridges, Academy Award–winning actor

*"Pen Densham's* Riding The Alligator *provides the essential tools of the trade and leaves more than sufficient room for individual creativity. His deep understanding of the screenwriting process is at once inspiring and empowering. An invaluable resource that is certain to become a must for all new screenwriters."*
        — Robert Mandel, Dean, AFI Conservatory

As principal of Trilogy Entertainment Group, PEN DENSHAM is an accomplished writer-director-producer. Pen created the story for the revisionist *Robin Hood: Prince of Thieves* and co-wrote and produced the screenplay with his Trilogy partner John Watson. He wrote and directed *Moll Flanders* for MGM, as well as writing and directing *Houdini* for TNT. Pen and Trilogy have produced 14 feature films.

**$24.95 · 280 PAGES · ORDER NUMBER 165RLS · ISBN: 9781932907841**

# THE SCRIPT-SELLNG GAME - 2ND ED.
## A HOLLYWOOD INSIDER'S LOOK AT GETTING YOUR SCRIPT SOLD AND PRODUCED

### KATHIE FONG YONEDA

Kathie Fong Yoneda

The Script-Selling Game is about what they never taught you in film school. This is a look at screenwriting from the other side of the desk — from a buyer who wants to give writers the guidance and advice that will help them to not only elevate their craft but to also provide them with the down-in-the-trenches information of what is expected of them in the script selling marketplace.

It's like having a mentor in the business who answers your questions and provides you with not only valuable information, but real-life examples on how to maneuver your way through the Hollywood labyrinth. While the first edition focused mostly on film and television movies, the second edition includes a new chapter on animation and another on utilizing the Internet to market yourself and find new opportunities, plus an expansive section on submitting for television and cable.

"I've been writing screenplays for over 20 years. I thought I knew it all — until I read The Script-Selling Game. The information in Kathie Fong Yoneda's fluid and fun book really enlightened me. It's an invaluable resource for any serious screenwriter."

> — Michael Ajakwe Jr., Emmy-winning TV producer, Talk Soup; Executive Director of Los Angeles Web Series Festival (LAWEBFEST); and creator/ writer/director of Who... and Africabby (AjakweTV.com)

"Kathie Fong Yoneda knows the business of show from every angle and she generously shares her truly comprehensive knowledge — her chapter on the Web and new media is what people need to know! She speaks with the authority of one who's been there, done that, and gone on to put it all down on paper. A true insider's view."

> — Ellen Sandler, former co-executive producer of Everybody Loves Raymond and author of The TV Writer's Workbook

KATHIE FONG YONEDA has worked in film and television for more than 30 years. She has held executive positions at Disney, Touchstone, Disney TV Animation, Paramount Pictures Television, and Island Pictures, specializing in development and story analysis of both live-action and animation projects. Kathie is an internationally known seminar leader on screenwriting and development and has conducted workshops in France, Germany, Austria, Spain, Ireland, Great Britain, Australia, Indonesia, Thailand, Singapore, and throughout the U.S. and Canada.

**$19.95 · 248 PAGES · ORDER NUMBER 161RLS · ISBN 13: 9781932907919**

# STORY LINE
## FINDING GOLD IN YOUR LIFE STORY

### JEN GRISANTI

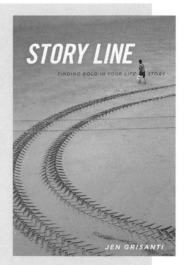

*Story Line: Finding Gold in Your Life Story* is a practical and spiritual guide to drawing upon your own story and fictionalizing it into your writing. As a Story Consultant and former VP of Current Programs at CBS/Paramount, most of the author's work with writers has focused on creating standout scripts by elevating story. The secret to telling strong story is digging deep inside yourself and utilizing your own life experiences and emotions to connect with the audience. As a television executive, the author asked writers about their personal stories and found that many writers had powerful life experiences, yet had surprisingly never drawn upon these for the sake of their writing because these experiences seemed to hit a little too close to home. This book is about jumping over that hurdle. The goal is not to write a straight autobiographical story which rarely transfers well. Rather, the intention is to dig deep into your well of experience, examine what you have inside, and use it to strengthen your writing. By doing so, you will be able to sell your scripts, find representation, be hired, and win writing competitions.

*"Jen Grisanti has spent her entire professional life around writers and writing. Her new book is nothing less than an instruction manual, written from her unique perspective as a creative executive, that seeks to teach neophyte writers how to access their own experiences as fuel for their television and motion picture scripts. It aspires to be for writers what 'the Method' is for actors."*

— Glenn Gordon Caron, writer/creator, *Moonlighting*, *Clean and Sober*, *Picture Perfect*, *Love Affair*, *Medium*

*"Jen Grisanti gets to the heart of what makes us want to be storytellers in the first place – to share something of ourselves and touch the spirits of others in the process. Her book is a powerful and compassionate guide to discovering and developing stories that will enable us to connect – with an audience and with each other."*

— Diane Drake, writer, *What Women Want*, *Only You*

JEN GRISANTI is a story consultant, independent producer, and the writing instructor for NBC's Writers on the Verge. She was a television executive for 12 years at top studios. She started her career in television and rose through the ranks of Current Programs at Spelling Television Inc. where Aaron Spelling was her mentor for 12 years.

**$26.95 · 250 PAGES · ORDER NUMBER 156RLS · ISBN 13: 9781932907896**

# THE WRITER'S JOURNEY – 3RD EDITION
## MYTHIC STRUCTURE FOR WRITERS

### CHRISTOPHER VOGLER

## *BEST SELLER*

See why this book has become an international best seller and a true classic. *The Writer's Journey* explores the powerful relationship between mythology and storytelling in a clear, concise style that's made it required reading for movie executives, screenwriters, playwrights, scholars, and fans of pop culture all over the world.

Both fiction and nonfiction writers will discover a set of useful myth-inspired storytelling paradigms (i.e., "The Hero's Journey") and step-by-step guidelines to plot and character development. Based on the work of Joseph Campbell, *The Writer's Journey* is a must for all writers interested in further developing their craft.

The updated and revised third edition provides new insights and observations from Vogler's ongoing work on mythology's influence on stories, movies, and man himself.

*"This book is like having the smartest person in the story meeting come home with you and whisper what to do in your ear as you write a screenplay. Insight for insight, step for step, Chris Vogler takes us through the process of connecting theme to story and making a script come alive."*
> – Lynda Obst, producer, *Sleepless in Seattle, How to Lose a Guy in 10 Days*;
> author, *Hello, He Lied*

*"This is a book about the stories we write, and perhaps more importantly, the stories we live. It is the most influential work I have yet encountered on the art, nature, and the very purpose of storytelling."*
> – Bruce Joel Rubin, screenwriter, *Stuart Little 2, Deep Impact,*
> *Ghost, Jacob's Ladder*

CHRISTOPHER VOGLER is a veteran story consultant for major Hollywood film companies and a respected teacher of filmmakers and writers around the globe. He has influenced the stories of movies from *The Lion King* to *Fight Club* to *The Thin Red Line* and most recently wrote the first installment of *Ravenskull*, a Japanese-style manga or graphic novel. He is the executive producer of the feature film *P.S. Your Cat is Dead* and writer of the animated feature *Jester Till*.

**$26.95 · 448 PAGES · ORDER NUMBER 76RLS · ISBN: 9781932907360**

# SAVE THE CAT!®
## THE LAST BOOK ON SCREENWRITING YOU'LL EVER NEED!

**BLAKE SNYDER**

## *BEST SELLER*

He made millions of dollars selling screenplays to Hollywood and here screenwriter Blake Snyder tells all. "Save the Cat!®" is just one of Snyder's many ironclad rules for making your ideas more marketable and your script more satisfying — and saleable, including:
- The four elements of every winning logline.
- The seven immutable laws of screenplay physics.
- The 10 genres and why they're important to your movie.
- Why your Hero must serve your idea.
- Mastering the Beats.
- Mastering the Board to create the Perfect Beast.
- How to get back on track with ironclad and proven rules for script repair.

This ultimate insider's guide reveals the secrets that none dare admit, told by a show biz veteran who's proven that you can sell your script if you can save the cat.

*"Imagine what would happen in a town where more writers approached screenwriting the way Blake suggests? My weekend read would dramatically improve, both in sellable/producible content and in discovering new writers who understand the craft of storytelling and can be hired on assignment for ideas we already have in house."*
> – From the Foreword by Sheila Hanahan Taylor, Vice President, Development at Zide/Perry Entertainment, whose films include *American Pie, Cats and Dogs, Final Destination*

*"One of the most comprehensive and insightful how-to's out there. Save the Cat!® is a must-read for both the novice and the professional screenwriter."*
> – Todd Black, Producer, *The Pursuit of Happyness, The Weather Man, S.W.A.T, Alex and Emma, Antwone Fisher*

*"Want to know how to be a successful writer in Hollywood? The answers are here. Blake Snyder has written an insider's book that's informative — and funny, too."*
> – David Hoberman, Producer, *The Shaggy Dog* (2005), *Raising Helen, Walking Tall, Bringing Down the House, Monk* (TV)

BLAKE SNYDER, besides selling million-dollar scripts to both Disney and Spielberg, was one of Hollywood's most successful spec screenwriters. Blake's vision continues on *www.blakesnyder.com*.

**$19.95 · 216 PAGES · ORDER NUMBER 34RLS · ISBN: 9781932907001**

# { THE MYTH OF MWP }

In a dark time, a light bringer came along, leading the curious and the frustrated to clarity and empowerment. It took the well-guarded secrets out of the hands of the few and made them available to all. It spread a spirit of openness and creative freedom, and built a storehouse of knowledge dedicated to the betterment of the arts.

The essence of the Michael Wiese Productions (MWP) is empowering people who have the burning desire to express themselves creatively. We help them realize their dreams by putting the tools in their hands. We demystify the sometimes secretive worlds of screenwriting, directing, acting, producing, film financing, and other media crafts.

By doing so, we hope to bring forth a realization of 'conscious media' which we define as being positively charged, emphasizing hope and affirming positive values like trust, cooperation, self-empowerment, freedom, and love. Grounded in the deep roots of myth, it aims to be healing both for those who make the art and those who encounter it. It hopes to be transformative for people, opening doors to new possibilities and pulling back veils to reveal hidden worlds.

MWP has built a storehouse of knowledge unequaled in the world, for no other publisher has so many titles on the media arts. Please visit www.mwp.com where you will find many free resources and a 25% discount on our books. Sign up and become part of the wider creative community!

Onward and upward,

Michael Wiese
Publisher/Filmmaker